VICTORY'S

TRIAL

By

Victoria Stehr

About The Author

Victoria Stehr, known as Vicky by her friends and family, is an extraordinary woman whose faith is the anchor of her life. She is a kind and compassionate soul with a great sense of humor who believes in the power of laughter to heal and uplift. For many years, Vicky has been honing her artistic skills, writing poetry, and creating beautiful drawings and paintings, with a particular fondness for horses, wildlife, and landscapes.

Vicky finds comfort in being close to nature and spending time with animals. The great outdoors rejuvenates her soul.

Vicky's career in social services is a shining example of her unwavering dedication to helping others. Over several decades, including 15 years in management, she has made a significant impact. Her passion for making a difference in people's lives is not just a job but a calling that drives her. Vicky's ultimate goal is to guide individuals toward inner peace and a fulfilling life, free from the burdens of mental illness, addictions, and traumas. Her faith in Jesus Christ is her guiding light, and she strives to share His love and compassion with everyone she meets.

Preface

Years back, a friend whose opinion I highly value suggested that I chronicle my life story by writing a book. At that moment, I felt that such a feat would be impossible to achieve and saw no reason for it. However, in 2015, a series of life-changing experiences made me realize the paramount importance and urgency of penning down my memoir.

Through the process of writing, I found healing and solace. It was through expressing my experiences via the written word that I found myself lifted and re-energized. My primary aim is to offer a helping hand to those who may be struggling in life and provide a deeper understanding of the challenges faced by those who suffer from mental illness.

Foreword

Victory's Trial by Victoria Stehr is a compelling memoir that takes readers on a journey of resilience, faith, and unwavering strength. As I immersed myself in the pages of this remarkable narrative, I was struck by the raw honesty and profound courage that Vicky demonstrates in recounting her most challenging and triumphant moments. Her ability to articulate the complexities of her experiences with mental illness, personal struggles, and her relentless pursuit of inner peace is truly extraordinary.

From the outset, Vicky opens her heart, inviting readers into the depths of her struggles with mental illness, personal challenges, and her quest for inner peace. Her story is a testament to the human spirit's resilience, healing, and ability to find hope in the darkest of times. She bravely confronts the painful details, allowing readers to empathize with the intensity of her emotions and the weight of her journey.

One of the most captivating aspects of *Victory's Trial* is Vicky's vivid storytelling. Each chapter offers a glimpse into her soul, revealing the pain she has endured and the victories she has achieved. From her early childhood memories to the moments of crisis and recovery, Vicky paints a poignant picture that is both heart-wrenching and inspiring. Her ability to find beauty amidst chaos is a testament to her indomitable spirit. Vicky's journey is not just her own; it is a beacon of light for anyone facing similar trials. Her vivid storytelling brings to life the highs and lows of her path, painting a picture that is both heart-wrenching and inspiring. Each chapter provides insight into the pain she has overcome and the triumphs she has experienced. She writes with clarity and honesty, offering a refreshing and deeply moving narrative. Her story is a powerful reminder that no matter how daunting the obstacles may seem, there is always a way forward.

Throughout her memoir, Vicky emphasizes the ignificance of faith and its role in her life. Her unwavering belief in a higher power has been her guiding light, giving her the strength to navigate through her darkest days. Her deep connection to nature, animals, and the healing power of art further underscores her resilience and her ability to find solace in the world around her. Vicky's descriptions of her artistic pursuits and her interactions with animals are particularly poignant, highlighting her capacity to find beauty and meaning even in the most challenging circumstances.

This book is dedicated to those who have struggled in silence, battled their demons, and continue to seek light in the darkness. Vicky's story is a powerful reminder that no matter how insurmountable the obstacles may seem, there is always a way forward. Her resilience is a testament to the strength that resides within us all. Her story serves as a beacon of hope, encouraging others to persevere, regardless of the challenges they face.

Victory's Trial also serves as an important educational resource, offering insights into the realities of living with mental illness. Vicky's candid account of her experiences imparts valuable lessons, fostering greater understanding and empathy for those confronting similar challenges. Her willingness to share her story with openness and vulnerability is a gift to all who read it.

As you delve into *Victory's Trial*, you will be moved by Vicky's unwavering faith and her profound connection to nature, animals, and the healing power of art. Her ability to find beauty and solace in the world around her, even in the face of adversity, is truly inspiring. Her descriptions of her artistic endeavors and her interactions with animals are particularly poignant, highlighting her capacity to find beauty and meaning in challenging circumstances. Her journey exemplifies the power of faith, love, and perseverance.

Victoria Stehr's courage and vulnerability in sharing her story are a gift to us all. Her memoir is not merely a personal account; it is a universal message of hope and resilience. May her experiences inspire and uplift you, reminding you that victory is always within reach, regardless of the trials you face. Her story is a powerful testament to our ability to overcome struggles and find a path to a brighter, more hopeful futureIn conclusion, I invite you to join Vicky on this profound journey. Walk alongside her as she navigates life's complexities and finds solace in her words. *Victory's Trial* is more than a memoir; it is a wellspring of hope, a guide for understanding, and a celebration of the triumph of the human spirit. Through her story, Vicky teaches us that even in our darkest moments, we can find light, and that with perseverance and faith, we can conquer any obstacle.

Julia Andrews

Award-winning actress

Table of Contents

Chapter 1

My World Fell Apart

1992

The events of Sunday, December 13th, are still vivid in my mind. I was standing in my sister Jen's kitchen, rambling nonsense to her, when my brother-in-law Cory walked in, looking confused. Suddenly, there was a knock on the back door, and a police officer walked in. He was tall and imposing, with bright red hair and dark glasses that gleamed in the light. He strode towards me, his hands on his hips, and said, *"You need to come with me."*

I was filled with terror and uncertainty, looking to Cory for reassurance. He simply said, *"It'll be alright."* But I had a nagging feeling that something was wrong. As I tried to run for the door, the police officer grabbed me with his large hands. I struggled and shouted, but it was no use. The fear and confusion were overwhelming.

It all happened so quickly. Cory, an avid wrestler, and the giant police officer wrestled me to the ground. I didn't give up, and I wouldn't go without a fight. I yelled, *"No, please, no!"* I cried, and fear welled up inside while the adrenaline rushed through my body. Two tall, powerful men outwrestled my 15-year-old body.

With my hands cuffed behind my back, the police officer escorted me outside to his squad car. The snow on the ground was thick and powdery. The air smelled of wood smoke and pine, and I could see my breath hanging in front of me. I felt horrified, ashamed, and in disbelief, questioning what I had done.

As I gazed through the squad car window, I caught a glimpse of my dad walking down the sidewalk on the opposite side of the street. Our eyes locked, and time seemed to stand still for a second. His face appeared to be contorted in anguish, and tears were streaming down his cheeks, leaving a glistening trail in their wake.

This was a cold December afternoon in '92, a typical winter day in Chisholm, Minnesota, with a bone-chilling gust of wind that makes your eyes water and your nose run. The sky was a bleak, gray color, and the sun was nowhere to be seen. That day, the cold was so intense that it seemed to seep into my bones, making me feel like I'd never be warm again.

As the holiday season loomed near, my heart remained devoid of joy. It seemed as though the weight of the world burdened my shoulders, leaving me to ponder whether happiness would ever find its way back to me.

Sadie Hawkins

Months before that dreaded December day, I was a typical 10th grader, or so I thought. I played on the high school volleyball team, had crushes on boys, liked music and animals, and wanted friends. Typical, right? But I felt odd and awkward around my peers.

Autumn is the season for Sadie Hawkins, the dance where the girl asks the boy. However, I wasn't interested in any of the boys in my grade, so I didn't give the dance much thought. That was until some girls claimed that a boy named Luke had expressed interest in me and wanted me to ask him to the dance. At first, I was doubtful and didn't believe them, but their persistent urging eventually convinced me to give it a shot.

One day, before my choir class, I saw Luke standing near the door of his next class, and my heart began to race. The girls had encouraged me to ask him out, so I sheepishly approached him and asked, *"Would you like to go to Sadie Hawkins with me?"* I remember feeling nervous and anxious, but to my surprise, Luke looked at me and said, *"Yes, sure, I do."*

On the day of Sadie Hawkins, my brother-in-law Cory videotaped Luke picking me up for the dance and the beginning of the event. Although Luke and I were both introverts, our personalities made the occasion a bit awkward. Despite this, Luke's kindness shone through, especially when he pulled his car closer to the sidewalk, likely to make it easier for me to get in. The ground was covered with snow, but I, in my shiny knee-high purple dress and black high heels, bravely trudged through the snow to get into his car.

We headed to the Wooden Table restaurant, situated north of Chisholm. Upon our arrival, a few other couples joined us. Luke and I sat across from each other, gazing out of the window and occasionally making eye contact. Our interactions were limited since he was shy and I was awkward. Before the dance, my brother-in-law Cory filmed the Sadie Hawkins groupies from above on the walkway in the old Chisholm High School gym before the dance started. Luke hung out with his buddies, leaving me to roam around like a lost puppy dog. I walked up to my childhood friend to say hi, but her friends quickly distracted her. I continued to stroll around, smiling and looking at anyone who would glance my way.

Recently, I watched the video that Cory had recorded from the evening of the Sadie Hawkins event; I couldn't help but feel a twinge of embarrassment. Seeing myself on screen, I realized how foolish I had looked as I wandered aimlessly around the room. My movements were hesitant and unsure, as if I were a lost puppy searching for its owner. It was a humbling experience.

As the dance music started playing, I took a seat at one of the tables and watched everyone else enjoy themselves. Luke was also sitting at the same table, engaged in a conversation with a friend.

Luke and I danced to a couple of slow songs while some classmates jeered, *"Is this loooove!"Woooow, look at you."* Feeling embarrassed and out of place, I just wanted to leave. Luke suggested going to someone's house for an "after-party," but I was neither a party-goer nor popular or well-liked.

At the house, people were drinking beer and urging me to join them. *"Drink, Vicky, drink!"*

"Come on, it'll be great!" But I declined, stating that I wasn't interested. One girl sat on Luke's lap while chugging down a beer and asked me, *"Does this bother you?"* I felt uncomfortable and shook my head, *"No."*

Upon returning home, my mom was still awake and asked me how my night went. Overwhelmed with emotions, I ran up to my room, crying. As my mom followed me to my room, I blurted out, *"It's not like anything happened!"* My mom sat on the bed beside me, trying to console me. I recounted how terrible the night had been and how I just wanted to go to bed. My mom listened attentively, likely concerned that the night wasn't what I had hoped for.

December

Imagine the relentless restlessness that keeps you awake through the night—a constant buzzing of excitement and creativity that refuses to grant you reprieve. That's precisely how I felt, my mind ablaze with ideas and visions that compelled me into action. Night after night, I found myself engrossed in crafting something new, a whirlwind of activity that left me both drained and invigorated.

I surrounded myself with an eclectic array of oddities in my room—plants, makeup, clothes, and stuffed animals arranged meticulously on my dresser. Hours were lost to experimenting with vibrant peach, purple, and blue eye makeup, each stroke fueling my enthusiasm for creation. Armed with my trusty 35mm camera, I snapped away, convinced that I was birthing a masterpiece with every click.

In my excitement, I couldn't contain myself, pouring out my thoughts to my mom, unable to complete sentences or make much sense. Yet, in those moments of frenzied expression, I found solace in the boundless energy of my creative pursuit, a force that refused to let me rest.

After nights of no sleep and overly excited activity, I visited my sister, Jen. It was December 13th, 1992, a cold winter day that matched my restless energy. I brought along a cassette tape of my favorite Christmas song, eager to share it with Jen. As the music played, I sang along, my voice rising and falling with the melody.

Noticed Jen walking into the room, holding her one-year-old son, Andrew. I couldn't help but notice the way he was moving on Jen's hip as she held him. *"Jen, why is Andrew humping you?"* I exclaimed. Jen stated, *"Vicky, he's just a baby bouncing up and down."* Despite my sister's attempts to calm me down, I couldn't help but feel restless. I stepped outside, and Jen followed me, barefooted in the freezing cold. *"Vicky, please come back inside, it'll be ok."* Everything seemed to be spiraling out of control, the calm winter day now replaced with chaos and confusion. December 13th, 1992, was the beginning of 'my frenzy' when I was wrestled and handcuffed.

Hospital

The towering police officer who escorted me to the hospital on that December day brought me into a blur of unfamiliar surroundings. The initial moments of my hospital stay are shrouded in a fog of uncertainty, but one memory stands out—a female nurse guiding me into a stark room furnished with only a bed, a wooden desk, and a solitary chair. She handed me a set of green clothes, urging me to change, but skepticism and fear held me back. I couldn't trust anyone in this bewildering situation, and her insistence only fueled my resistance.

So, I adamantly refused, but the nurse insisted that I change. Eventually, two chubby male nurses walked in - one with a shaggy brownish beard and the other with balding dark hair.

The two male nurses stood out due to their impressive size and prominence in the room. The one said, *"You need to change into these clothes; you don't have a choice."* I was so scared and wouldn't, just couldn't do it. Next thing, they were pulling my clothes off of me piece by piece while I struggled and fought to stay dressed. My shirt, bra, underwear, pants, socks, and shoes were torn off. They force-dressed me as I continued to wail as my body went limp. I lay there on the bed gasping as I slowly stopped crying. I didn't know what was happening; I wanted to go home.

Lying there in the sterile hospital room, surrounded by the unfamiliar hum of medical machinery and the faint echoes of distant voices, I felt like a lost soul adrift in a sea of uncertainty. Abruptly, the door groaned open, admitting a female nurse who bore a weighty stack of papers and a plain pencil. Without any explanation, she deposited the papers onto the worn wooden desk with a thud, commanding, *"Complete this test."*

Reluctantly, I mustered the strength to rise from the bed, settling onto the unsteady wooden chair, my gaze fixed upon the daunting multiple-choice questions sprawled before me. Each query seemed to blur into the next, a labyrinth of incomprehensible words and concepts that mocked my frazzled mind. Despite my efforts, the answers remained elusive, slipping through my grasp like sand through clenched fingers.

Defeated and overwhelmed, I surrendered to the oppressive weight of the moment, sinking back into the hospital bed. In that solitary instant, enveloped by the silence of my own thoughts, felt the crushing weight of isolation and helplessness descend upon me.

The nurse returned to my room, briefly shuffling the papers on the desk before turning her attention to me. Without much thought, she handed me a small paper cup filled with water and a couple of pills placed in a wafer cup. Still reeling from the day's events, I didn't bother to ask any questions and obediently took the pills.

As the medicine kicked in, my mind began to quiet down, and I drifted off to sleep, lying under the soft, blush-colored blanket. Suddenly, an old, frumpy, limping man entered the room, dragging one foot behind him. He was bald with a prominent nose, and he looked ancient. *"Hello, I am Dr. Leroy. I see you didn't finish your questions,"* he said, trying to engage me in conversation. However, I was still dazed and barely responded.

Dr. Leroy's questions blurred together in a hazy fog; their meaning lost in the tumult of my thoughts. With each inquiry, my confusion deepened, and uncertainty bore down upon me like an impossible burden. After a while, he shuffled out of the room, leaving me alone with my thoughts. Panic and fear rushed through my soul as I tried to make sense of why I was there. All I wanted was to go home.

The Room

The events leading up to my arrival in that bleak small room are a complete blur. I can't remember the circumstances that brought me there. All I know is that when I came to, I was disoriented and struggling to make sense of my surroundings. As I recall, I was guided to a dimly lit room, my head spinning and my steps faltering. The room was bare except for a flat, thin gray mat I was asked to lie on. The walls were covered in dark padded plastic mats, which gave off a musty smell. As I lay there, my emotions overtook me, and I couldn't help but cry. I waited anxiously, my mind racing with questions and worries. Despite my exhaustion, I couldn't find peace and lay there, restless and unsettled.

Lost in fear and isolation, I felt punished and alone. Tears flowed as I wondered where my parents were and if I had done something wrong. Time dragged on, each moment an eternity. I feared I'd never see my family again, forgotten and abandoned. I didn't trust anyone; suspicion poisoned my mind. Why was I in a padded room with only a flat mat? What was happening to me?

My heart soared with hope at the gentle knock on the door, signaling my mom's arrival; as the nurse ushered her in, tears of relief cascaded down my cheeks, her presence a comfort in the rigid hospital environment. I asked, *"Mom? Is it really you?"* *"Vicky, oh Vicky, I'm here for you. I even made you your favorite sandwich, bologna on white bread."* My mom replied.

Yet, when she offered it to me, I hesitated, unable to trust even the simplest gestures of care. Mistrust gripped me tightly, convinced that even the food before me was tainted.

"Vicky, they said I have to go, I'm sorry." as tears fell down my mom's face. I looked at her in disbelief, saying, *"No, please take me home."*

In the suffocating confines of the padded room, isolation weighed heavily upon me, the walls closing in with each passing moment. Despite my mother's presence just beyond the threshold, I remained trapped within the confines of my solitude, unable to bridge the distance between us. With no escape from the relentless grip of confinement, I surrendered to the overwhelming tide of despair, my tears mingling with the silence of the night as sleep offered temporary respite from the turmoil within.

I woke up dazed and confused. Where was I, I thought. My mind cleared, and I realized how badly I had to pee. I pounded on the padded door, peering through the tiny square window and yelling for help. *"Please, please help me! I have to go!"*

No answer, no sound, just silence. Was this it? Was I going to be left here to die? What did I do? Why? Why didn't anyone come? I gave up after pounding and pounding and crying for help. I laid back down on the thin gray mat, tears rolling down my cheeks. prayed, *"Dear Lord, please help me."* My bladder was ready to burst, but no one ever came to the door. This was it. I couldn't hold it anymore. The warmth of the urine pooled around me on the pad, spilling onto the floor.

The warm urine grew cold, and I lay there ashamed and afraid. Finally, a nurse came to check on me. I said, *"I just couldn't hold it. I had to go so bad!"* The nurse escorted me back to my old room, stating, *"Here's a towel and soap; take a shower."*

A week into my hospital stay, my cousin visited me, her troubled countenance evident as tears streaked down her cheeks. *"Vicky, I'm so sorry,"* she murmured, her voice heavy with regret. Bewildered, I struggled to comprehend the depth of her apology. Was she expressing sorrow for my circumstances, or was there something more she wished to convey? To this day, I don't recall the full conversation. I just remember her tears and apologizing.

As I sat there pondering my cousin's visit, a nurse placed a plate of homemade white chocolate candies in the dining area. The sweet aroma filled the room, and I couldn't resist biting. The candy was divine, and I could not stop eating it. The holiday season was just around the corner, and this small gesture brought a glimmer of joy to my otherwise dreary hospital stay.

I experienced an unexpected period during my time there, and I was unprepared for it. To make matters worse, my clothes were green, and I could not protect them. I was not allowed to wear underwear. Fortunately, the nurse on duty was kind enough to provide me with a pad. However, it was a giant pad, and I had no choice but to stick it to my pants. The entire experience was very uncomfortable and embarrassing.

One evening, my mom and dad visited me. My mom handed me a small floral pink gift bag and said, *"Vicky, look inside."* As I opened the bag, I found a pewter bear with a pendant on it. The pendant looked like a diamond.

My mom said, *"Vicky, you're so precious, just like this bear. It has the same stone on it as your birthstone, the diamond. You're as strong and precious as a diamond."*

During another visit from my mom, I overheard her conversation with a nurse. She expressed concern about my slow walking and zombie-like stare and asked if it would improve over time. The nurse responded reassuringly, saying she was confident everything would be alright.

I just wanted to leave and go home from the hospital. I saw people entering and exiting through big metal doors, probably doctors, nurses, or visitors. I waited for a moment when no nurse was around and quickly went through the doors, even though my movements were so slow. I thought I had finally escaped and could go home. However, a large male nurse with dark black hair appeared in front of me and asked me where I thought I was going. He then told me to go back inside.

Every day in the hospital followed a monotonous routine. Mornings began with the ritual of rising, queuing up at the nurses' station for medication, and partaking in a mundane breakfast. Group therapy sessions punctuated the day, where discussions revolved around strategies for improvement, followed by a brief respite for rest. Lunch provided a fleeting break from the monotony before the cycle repeated itself: another round of medication, another meal, and finally, the quiet descent into sleep. Each day blended into the next, a relentless procession of monotony that left me longing for a semblance of variety and excitement.

A cocktail, yum yum, colorful, small ones, big ones, swallow them down! Why do I take them? To slow me down! To make me sleep all day long, all night long. Take them, take them, or you'll never leave. Yum yum yum, as they go down.

As I gathered my belongings and prepared to depart, a rush of liberation flooded my senses, as if emerging from a long and arduous journey. The stifling atmosphere of the hospital dissolved in the wake of newfound freedom, replaced by the refreshing fragrance of the outside world. Stepping into the crisp air, I left behind the stagnant confines of the hospital, embracing the promise of returning home to the warmth of familiar faces and cherished surroundings.

Discharged on December 23rd, 1992, I returned home with a mix of emotions. Despite the comfort of familiar surroundings, the effects of medication weighed heavily upon me. Throughout the day, I lay on the couch, enveloped in a haze induced by medication, my body rendered inert by its potent effects.

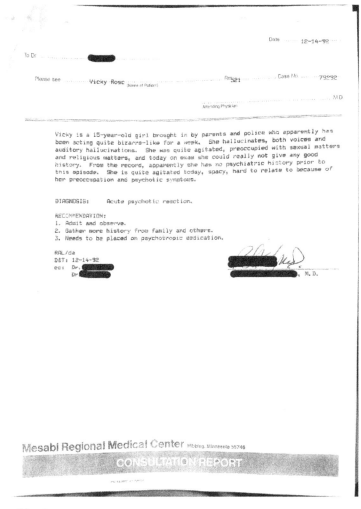

Vicky is a 15-year-old girl brought in by parents and police who apparently has been acting quite bizarre-like for a week. She hallucinates, both voices and auditory hallucinations. She was quite agitated, preoccupied with sexual matters and religious matters, and today on exam she could really not give any good history. From the record, apparently she has no psychiatric history prior to this episode. She is quite agitated today, spacy, hard to relate to because of her preoccupation and psychotic symptoms.

DIAGNOSIS: Acute psychotic reaction.

RECOMMENDATION:
1. Admit and observe.
2. Gather more history from family and others.
3. Needs to be placed on psychotropic medication.

RAL/da
D&T: 12-14-92
cc: Dr.
     Dr

Mesabi Regional Medical Center Hibbing, Minnesota 55746

CONSULTATION REPORT

Side effects

Experiencing lockjaw, I found myself grappling with a perplexing and distressing phenomenon: my jaw would suddenly remain wide open after attempting to speak, leaving me immobilized for moments before regaining control. Eating became a challenge, and exhaustion weighed heavily as I retreated into periods of deep slumber. In addition to the unsettling jaw symptoms, my legs trembled with uncontrollable intensity, adding further strain to my already burdened state.

"David!" I'd yell, *"Come over here and sit on my legs; help your big sis."*

David was about nine years old at the time. He came running, sitting on my legs, giggling nervously. My legs wouldn't stop squirming from the tremors. David tried his best to calm my shaking legs. I liked having my brother hang out with me.

Days passed by while I lay there on the couch, jaw locking, legs kicking, eyes glazed over. Mornings, when David was getting ready for school, he'd yell, *"Mom, she's staring at me again!"*

He was standing in the dining room across the room. I never meant to. Poor David was scared of seeing his big sister like this. I lay there staring, drooling, and just out of it.

That December, winter arrived with its customary ferocity, blanketing the landscape in snow and enveloping us in bone-chilling cold. Despite its familiarity, this winter carried a unique significance. The relentless weather did not stop my brother-in-law Cory from building a towering snowman reaching an impressive 20 feet in height. His remarkable achievement garnered attention from the local newspaper, earning him a coveted spot on the front page.

Amidst the bitter winds and icy temperatures, the Open Door church, where I worshiped, underwent a transformation. Despite the inhospitable conditions, the construction team persisted and, against all odds, completed the church's construction at its new location, just in time for its grand opening.

Regrettably, the memories of Christmas 1992 elude me. The sights, sounds, and scents of the holiday season remain lost in the fog of forgotten moments. It's as if that Christmas never happened, and I can't help but feel a sense of loss when I think about it.

The year 1992 stands out in my memory as a turning point in my life. It was a tumultuous time filled with significant events that left a lasting impact on me. I can still vividly recall the details of that year, like a picture carved into a solid slab of stone, forever etched in my mind. The events of 1992 changed me in ways I never anticipated, and I still feel the effects of that year to this day.

The pox

During a visit to my sister Jen's house in January 1993 with my mom, my niece Angela, who was three years old at the time, was lying in the living room with chickenpox - a common ailment for toddlers at her age. While my sister and mom spent time visiting in the kitchen, I didn't think twice and picked up Angela as I always did, being her aunt.

A few weeks later, I noticed a pimple on the tip of my nose, just above my right nostril. Initially dismissing it as a common occurrence, I attempted to squeeze it. However, my efforts proved futile as another pimple surfaced on my forehead, followed by one below my ribs. With growing discomfort and itching, the dreadful realization dawned upon me—I had contracted chickenpox.

The ensuing days unfolded into a nightmarish ordeal. The pain was excruciating, leaving me utterly drained and debilitated. The relentless itching felt like torture, my skin ablaze with discomfort. Coupled with fever and overall malaise, each moment seemed an eternity. Reflecting on the situation, I regretted not being more cautious around my niece, realizing the consequences of my oversight.

Navigating the psychotropic side effects of medication added a layer of frustration to the already challenging experience. As a teenager, I found myself questioning the unfairness of it all. Having never contracted chickenpox as a baby, I grappled with the harsh reality of the illness. Despite attempts to alleviate the discomfort with oatmeal baths and various remedies, relief remained elusive. In the end, only time would offer respite from the relentless affliction.

I was just hospitalized for God knows what, given these crazy medications, and finally getting used to most of the side effects and dealing with this! I missed so much school already. I was out of school for three weeks before getting chicken pox. Now,

I would be missing more school. I do not wish chickenpox on any teenager, ever.

My mom attended my first check-up with Dr. Leroy on February 3rd, 1993. She was always my advocate and protective of me, at least. Her unwavering support and protective nature provided solace amidst the uncertainty. She voiced concerns about the severe side effects I experienced, prompting adjustments to my medication regimen. The alleviation of these side effects was a relief, sparing me from potential long-term complications such as permanent ticks, lip smacks, or even jaw-locking—manifestations of Tardive Dyskinesia, a chilling reminder of the risks posed by certain psychotropic medications.

Grateful for the reprieve from these harrowing side effects, I couldn't help but ponder the potential consequences had adjustments not been made. The specter of Tardive Dyskinesia loomed large, a sobering reminder of the profound impact that medication choices can have on one's life.

School

I went back to school on February 8th, 1993. Some classmates asked where I'd been. I just shrugged, saying things like, *"I was sick,"* or *"I got chicken pox."* I was far behind; so many classes and assignments I missed. True to her nature, Mom took charge and called the school to explain my situation, or at least, I believe she did. Her proactive approach ensured that the school accommodated my missed classes, allowing me to bypass the educational setbacks caused by my health challenges.

I don't remember much about 10th grade except the lingering side effects. After taking my morning medication, I would get so nauseous. Mom would drive me to school, and she'd pull over while I opened the door before the car even stopped. I threw up. Mom would say,

"You, ok? You want to go back home?"

"Yes," I would respond. I'd go home and sleep the day away.

I vividly recall feeling a sense of pity or guilt emanating from my mom toward me. However, I never quite understood the reason behind it. Even after all these years, I remain uncertain about what fueled her desire to protect me. But one thing was sure - her love for me was the primary driving force behind her actions. My mom always looked out for my well-being and wanted nothing but the best for me. However, in retrospect, I realize that she may have been codependent or somewhat of a *'helicopter parent.'* Although the term wasn't in currency back in the 90s, it is a commonly used phrase nowadays.

"In every situation I encountered,
I found strength and comfort in the unwavering presence of Jesus
within my heart."
The steadfast love of the Lord never ceases; his mercies never come to an end; they are new every morning; great is your faithfulness. The Lord is my portion, says my soul; therefore, I will hope in him. - Lamentations 3:22-24

Chapter 2

High school Reality

Summer '93

During the blissful, sun-kissed months, I would eagerly hop on my trusty bike and head towards the wooden park or spend hours fishing alongside my dad. When I wasn't out and about, I would spend lazy afternoons lounging at home with my furry companions, relishing their warm company. But, the highlight of my summer was undoubtedly my horse Flicka. I would make regular trips to the quaint little township of Balkan, which is nestled just north of Chisholm, to visit and ride my majestic filly. It was a season that felt like any other, except for the strange, mysterious medication concoction that I was taking during that time.

I had a paper route to help pay for the fees of boarding my beloved horse, Flicka. Despite my efforts, my mom always seemed worried about our family finances and the cost of keeping Flicka. She never explicitly said it, but her actions spoke volumes. I could sense her reluctance to help me pay for Flicka's board. One day, while riding Flicka at a horse show in Balkan, my heart sank as it was announced that she was for sale. I knew that Flicka was an excellent gaming horse, and a lady wanted her for her daughter. The day came for Flicka to be sold, and as I wrapped my arm round her neck, tears streamed down my face. Riding Flicka was my one source of happiness; now she was gone. My world had suddenly become a lot less colorful. No more horse, no more joy.

Flicka and me at a horse show

As I rode the bus to a summer youth event, the sweltering heat made me restless. I decided to strike up a conversation with some girls I considered friends. Hoping to connect with them, I opened up about my December experiences. I spoke candidly about the struggles I faced in 10th grade, not knowing that this would only exacerbate my already challenging teenage life. Despite my best intentions, the heat was not the only thing that made me feel uneasy on that bus ride.

On summer nights, downtown Chisholm buzzed with the energy of teenagers hanging around, chatting, laughing, and enjoying their freedom. Some rode their bicycles around town, while others played hacky sacks, showing off their skills. It was a place where they could be themselves, away from the watchful eyes of parents and teachers. However, for me, it was a different story. I often felt like an outsider trying to fit in. One night, while I was in the middle of the crowd, a boy who was a year older suddenly yelled, *"Vicky Rosc, the psychotic bitch!"* as he ran across the main street. I froze in shock, not knowing how to react or respond. I felt embarrassed and hurt, and the incident left a lasting impact on me.

Junior Year '93 -'94

As I entered my junior year of high school, I couldn't help but feel a sense of excitement, knowing that graduation was just around the corner. The familiar routine of volleyball practice in August brought back memories of the previous year, and I was eager to return to the court. As for my electives, I stuck with my tried-and-true choices of art and choir, which had always been a source of joy and creativity for me. With so much to look forward to, I couldn't wait to see what the year had in store.

In the school hallways, it was common for some kid to yell out *"Pyscho!"* in a mocking tone as I walked by. As an office aid, when I would collect the absentee slips from different classes, a group of students would start chanting, *"PSYCHO!"* at the top of their lungs, drawing attention to me. The class would then erupt in laughter, and everyone would point and stare at me in an uncomfortable and degrading manner.

As I navigated the bustling school hallways, I couldn't ignore the hushed whispers and stifled giggles trailing in my wake. The disdainful glances from some of the girls made me feel as though I were the most loathsome person alive. Whether in class, transitioning between periods, or boarding the bus home, the weight of judgmental stares and mocking laughter seemed inescapable. Gradually, the murmurs morphed into malicious rumors, with clusters of girls conspiring in hushed tones about me, as if I were invisible. Their venomous words cut deep, leaving wounds too painful to recount. It felt as though I had unwittingly become a target, an easy prey for those seeking to spread callous gossip. Before I knew it, being called names like psycho, crazy, stupid, and worse had become a part of my everyday life. It was like a dark cloud had settled over me, following me wherever I went, and I couldn't seem to shake it off.

Girl's lockers were separate from boy's lockers. Some girl thought it would be funny to write PSYCHO on my locker while I was at lunch. It was smeared on my entire locker.

Back in the 1990s, kids used to tease and taunt each other, but the term "bullying" was not as widely used as it is today. As for me, I was unfortunately a target of bullying in my junior year of high school. It was a harrowing experience for me to go through, it made me feel isolated, sad, and afraid. The constant harassment and belittling were not something I could quickly shake off, and it affected my self-esteem and confidence.

The only break I got during school was when I went to Nanny's house for lunch. Nanny was my sanctuary, a haven in the storm. Her home was a place where I could relax and refuel, which helped me get through the rest of the day. Unfortunately, Nanny became ill and could no longer have me over for lunch. Though I was sad to leave, I was grateful for my time with her. Her kindness and love had given me the strength to face whatever challenges lay ahead. Her Sicilian spark and her warm hugs still inspire me to face life with a smile and a laugh, regardless of the situation.

High school was a tumultuous time for me. It felt like the drama would never stop. I was constantly being called names and sneered at, and I didn't know how to react or what to do in those situations. My default response was giggling nervously, even though my self-esteem was taking a hit. It was a daily struggle to deal with the negative comments and attitudes of my peers.

After school, I would come home feeling exhausted and defeated. I would lay on my bed, replaying the day's events in my head, and cry. I tried my best to be nice to everyone, friendly, kind, and fun. I felt like I needed to be more liked and more accepted in order to fit in and be happy.

As I walked into class, I heard some girls calling me by a name I didn't recognize. When I asked them why they were calling me Kimmy, one of the girls replied sarcastically, *"Because you're annoying, just like the girl on TV!"* Another girl would tease me, saying, *"Vicky, you're so slow."* I tried to defend myself by putting on a brave face and saying, *"No, I'm not slow. Watch me!"* I would then run up the hall stairs, skipping each step to show my speed. She would laugh, and her friend would join in the fun while I tried to brush off their remarks. *"Vicky, you're slow because you don't know anything!"* Her friend would say mockingly.

These interactions left me feeling confused and hurt. I always tried to be friendly, kind, and empathetic to everyone, but others didn't like me. My junior year was challenging, and it only brought me down. I often wished I could just disappear, move away, or hide under a rock. I tried to make sense of it all, but I just couldn't.

As I reminisce about my junior year of volleyball, I recall the constant feeling of not fitting in. Despite playing the sport since junior high, I had a terrible time. I felt like an outsider, as if I didn't belong on the team. Even worse, the assistant coach seemed to have a problem with me. Every time I stepped onto the court, I felt like I was walking on eggshells. It was an uncomfortable situation to be in, and I was miserable.

Homecoming wasn't the joyous celebration I had hoped for. During the volleyball homecoming nickname ceremony, I was given a nickname that wasn't fun or nice. The other girls on the team were given amusing nicknames, but mine was *"Vicky: I know,"* Rosc. While I'm sure the girls didn't mean any harm, the nickname only served to make me feel even more like an outcast. I had a habit of saying *"I know"* to the coach when he told me to do something, but I only said it to let him know that I had heard him. It was a small gesture of acknowledgment.

Finishing my junior year

Despite my best efforts to hide it, I was going through a tough time. I didn't have any friends, and my peers constantly picked on me. I felt like I didn't fit in anywhere. Even at youth group, where I was supposed to feel supported and welcomed, I struggled to connect with others. My behavior was probably off-putting to some people. Still, I was trying to cope with my feelings of isolation and loneliness. It wasn't until years later that I found out the youth pastor from my church had been struggling to figure out how to help me; he said he didn't know how to handle my behavior. It was a difficult time.

During my attempts to integrate into another church's youth group, one visit turned distressing. I wore white pants and a long-sleeved V-neck tight T-shirt with a pattern. A teenage boy accused me of leading him on with my outfit, prompting him to complain to the tall youth pastor. Unfortunately, the youth pastor showed no sympathy, reprimanding me for wearing what he deemed inappropriate clothing. Devastated, I left in tears, never intending to mislead anyone with my attire.

High school can be a challenging time for most people, and I can attest to that. The teasing and bullying I endured during those years were tough, but they also helped me build resilience as a person. While I have always wanted to attend high school reunions, I have never felt the need to do so. I never really connected with anyone during that time, and as a result, I never felt any desire to reconnect with my peers. That being said, I hold no grudges against anyone, and I believe that forgiveness is essential for emotional growth and development. Perhaps, I will attend my next class reunion, but I am still unsure.

During my junior year, I grappled with overwhelming sadness. Without friends to confide in, I faced the added blow of relinquishing my cherished horse due to financial strain. It felt as though I was sinking into a pit of despair, with each day marked by lethargy and an inability to focus.

The absence of companionship compounded my sense of isolation, leaving me to question whether anyone truly cared about my well-being.

In response to relentless bullying, my dad took a stand, meeting with the school principal to address the constant name-calling and rumors plaguing my school life. He hoped for decisive action from the administration, but unfortunately, the principal's promises remained unfulfilled. Despite my dad's earnest efforts, the bullying persisted, leaving me feeling helpless and overlooked in the face of adversity.

The arrival of summer filled me with joy and relief. The warmth of the sun and the extended daylight hours brought a renewed sense of optimism and positivity. I eagerly anticipated the opportunities and experiences this new season would bring, marking the start of a fresh chapter in my life. With enthusiasm, I looked forward to exploring new avenues and embracing unfamiliar experiences. Ready to confront any challenges that arose, I was determined to make the most of this beautiful time of year and seize the opportunities it presented.

"Turmoil in my soul, anguish, and fear,
yet my one true friend, Jesus, would always draw near."
The Lord is near to the brokenhearted and saves the crushed in spirit. - Psalm 34:18

Chapter 3

A shift

Is there hope?

My senior year was rapidly approaching, and I couldn't help but feel a lack of excitement within my soul. Looking back on those past two years, it was hard not to feel like I was living under a perpetual cloud. It seemed as though every day was shrouded in an unshakeable gloom, like a thick fog that refused to lift. The weight of it all was heavy on my shoulders, and I often struggled to find a way out of the darkness. Flicka, my beloved horse no longer my sanctuary; there was no point in joining volleyball and having no friends; this was it, nothing. But *maybe* something brighter was in store for me.

On the first day of my senior year, I was already struggling after a problematic year before. Most seniors had chosen home-ec as an elective to have an excellent way to finish high school. In the home-ec class, there were square tables with four chairs. When I tried to sit down at the table where a few girls I hung out with in the past were sitting, two of whom I considered friends at the time, the third girl said while grabbing the chair, *"No, we're just going to have the three of us sit here."* I looked at the other two, but they didn't respond.

Feeling sad, I walked to the back of the room, where one table was left with only one guy sitting there. I quietly sat beside him, but my heart was filled with sadness. It turned out that my friends weren't really my friends after all. However, over time, it didn't matter. The guy I shared the table with was a good cook and showed me a few tricks. I remember him teaching me how to crack eggs quickly. He gleamed as he shared how to do this because he worked at a restaurant in town.

Driving

One spring day, I experienced a situation where I woke up feeling unwell and decided to stay home from school. However, as the day progressed, I started feeling better and decided to go to school after lunch. Since I didn't have my own car, I reached out to my sister Jen and her husband Cory to ask if I could borrow one of their vehicles. Cory offered me their 4-wheel drive Eagle station wagon, even though it was an unattractive brown color.

As I drove towards the school in the station wagon, I attempted to roll down the windows to let in some fresh air, but I couldn't seem to locate the handles. While I was distracted, I glanced upwards and noticed I was approaching a tree. Unfortunately, I didn't have enough time to react. I collided with the tree, causing me to hit my head on the windshield, which spider-webbed on impact. I wasn't wearing a seatbelt.

As I sat in the car, a man opened his back door; I hit a tree on the boulevard next to his house. The man was my driver's ed teacher. How ironic! An ambulance was called, even though I thought I was okay. But my family figured it would be best for me to be checked just in case. Thankfully, I had no significant injuries and was released to go home.

Because I wasn't wearing a seatbelt, the police made me watch a safety video on driving with a seatbelt. To this day, I always buckle up. Cory teased me for a while because I totaled his vehicle with which he planned to go to Montana.

As I reminisce, I can still envision the Ash tree I collided with. Recently, I drove past that house to check if the tree still bore any marks from the accident. However, I was disappointed to find out that Chisholm had cut down most of the trees lining the streets, including the one I hit. Nonetheless, the house of my driver's ed instructor remains unaltered.

Rays of Sunshine

It was a regular day when I had to babysit my younger brother David and his friends at his birthday celebration at the local bowling alley on Saturday, November 5th. It was a quiet atmosphere, except for my brother's group, who were busy having fun. Amidst all the noise and excitement, I saw a charming blue-eyed guy with glasses behind the counter with a friendly smile. Something about him attracted me; his pleasant demeanor and   warm smile made me feel comfortable around him. I couldn't resist the temptation to flirt with him, and to my surprise, he seemed to enjoy my company, too.

As the evening progressed, I found myself distracted from my babysitting duties, and my poor brother had to come and get me or yell, *"Vicky, it's your turn to bowl!"* because I was too busy flirting with the blue-eyed guy. I couldn't resist; I asked him out on a date, and to my delight, he agreed. That's when my senior year became much brighter.

The blue-eyed guy, Scott, turned out to be everything I could ask for - sweet, kind, and fun to be around. We hit it off instantly and enjoyed spending time together, whether it was playing/watching sports, playing Nintendo, listening to music, hanging out at the bowling alley, hunting, or attending family gatherings. We managed to spend a lot of time together. I would go to the bowling alley while he participated in the league on Mondays and Wednesdays. On Saturday nights, I would hang out with him while he worked. We even attended each other's churches on Sundays, Open Doors, and Our Saviour Lutheran.

Scott was a good guy, intelligent, athletic, and tender. He had a great sense of humor and always knew how to make me laugh. I knew I had found someone truly amazing. We were both good kids, and together, we made the most of my senior year. Scott was my ray of sunshine.

My senior year was so much better now that Scott was in my life. I felt content and fulfilled with my art, and I managed adequately in my other classes. I had a few female acquaintances I sat with during lunch, and we sang together in choir. They were all pleasant to be around.

Spring was fast approaching, and it was time for prom. Most seniors attend prom, but after chatting with Scott about it, we decided to skip the dance and partying and attend the post-prom instead. It was a fun overnight stay in the school gym. We had a blast playing cards and basketball and even swam in the pool. It was a night to remember.

As I looked at the date on my calendar, I was reminded of the day I met Scott. It was on November 5th, which happens to be Guy Fawkes Day, a British celebration that commemorates the failure of the Gunpowder Plot of 1605. Guy Fawkes and his group had attempted to blow up the Houses of Parliament during that time. The coincidence that Scott's surname is Fawkes made this day even more fascinating to me. The irony of the situation was not lost on me and I can't help but appreciate it.

Graduation 1995

Towards the end of my senior year, a wave of excitement and anticipation engulfed me as I looked forward to my impending graduation, my boyfriend, and a future full of opportunities. However, the pressure, excitement, and stress of the approaching end of my school year eventually took a toll on me. I cannot recall the exact sequence of events, but I found myself admitted to the hospital in May, just a few days before my graduation ceremony. As a result, I missed a couple of final exams and almost missed my graduation. The hospital room was all too familiar, with the same blush-colored blanket that I had seen back in 1992 and hospitalized due to me missing for several hours and apparently going on a shopping spree. While in the hospital, I rambled on about my future plans incoherently.

Before I graduated, my mom decided to renovate our kitchen. She had a habit of remodeling whenever we hosted significant events at our place. I remember helping demolish everything and getting overly excited about the whole process. However, the next thing I knew, I was in the hospital. Dr. Leroy again, and this time, he added Tegretol to my list of medications. He let me be discharged so I could make it to my graduation ceremony.

The ceremony could have been more exciting, just a typical graduation event. However, our class decided to make it unique by having the girls wear green, and the guys wear silver for their gowns. How ironic! Green! Just like my hospital clothes. Our school colors are red and blue, but our class wanted to break away from the norm.

I had a fantastic graduation party! My closest relatives, a few classmates, our neighbors, and, of course, Scott made it to the party. The weather was perfect on a pleasant June day, the sun shining brightly and a slight breeze blowing. I borrowed Cory's video camera and went around the party, capturing every moment on video. However, I must admit that my voice was hoarse from talking too much in the weeks leading up to the party. I was too enthusiastic while filming some of my family members, which could have been annoying. Later, my mom confided in me that she was grateful that I was in the hospital so she and everyone else could get things done without feeling a bit overwhelmed by me.

As the graduation party came to an end, I found myself drawn to my favorite tree, the Mountain Ash tree, in the front yard. Memories flooded my mind of carefree days spent climbing its sturdy branches and hanging upside down with my childhood friends. With a sense of childlike wonder, I climbed up into its welcoming embrace. I frenziedly yelled out to Scott, *"Come on,*

Climb up here!"

Scott joined me in the tree as the sun began to set. We sat perched on the tree, taking in the beauty of the world around us. I suggested we take a walk, and although Scott may have been ready to call it a day, he humored me. We headed towards Long Year Lake on the other side of town. The trail around the lake was serene and peaceful, with the calm waters reflecting the beauty of the surrounding trees and night sky. As we walked, I chatted about my hopes and dreams and felt warmth and comfort in his presence. As we reached the end of the trail, we stopped to admire the Fountain on the island across the way, with its colorful lights dancing on the water in a mesmerizing display. At that moment, I was filled with a deep appreciation for the beauty of nature and the joy of sharing it with someone I cared about deeply. Scott was indeed a wonderful and sweet man, and I felt grateful to have him in my life.

College

Amidst the fall season of 1995, as the leaves transformed into a vibrant display of colors and the air became cooler, Scott enrolled in Hibbing Community College, eagerly pursuing a degree in mechanical design. Meanwhile, I, too, was attending college at the time, driven more by a desire to be close to Scott than by any sense of career direction. Although my college memories are somewhat hazy, I distinctly recall thriving in courses that allowed me to express my creativity and connect with others. My favorites were interpersonal communication, art, theater, and choir courses. I enjoyed participating in other courses, especially the Cardinal volleyball team I joined that fall, relishing the opportunity to test my skills on the court. However, it was my involvement in theater that truly set my heart alight. I spent countless hours backstage, working tirelessly to ensure each production went off without a hitch. From arranging the stage equipment to managing the stage lighting, I was fully committed to making sure that everything ran smoothly. And when I wasn't behind the scenes, I was on stage, belting out tunes and twirling across the stage in the musical Tommy, a highlight of my college experience.

1996

I recall a particular instance when I was consumed by a longing to see my boyfriend, Scott. Driven by my intense emotion, I visited him at his family's home. The night was dark and silent, and the only sound that could be heard was the crisp snow under my feet. Finally, I reached his house and knocked on the door with increasing urgency.

To my dismay, my knocking had woken up his dad, who had fainted while answering the door. The scene was quite chaotic, with Scott's mother rushing to his aid. Meanwhile, I stood there feeling guilty and helpless, realizing that my impulsive actions had caused this disruption.

Due to my behavior that night and previous days, police were contacted, and I was brought to the emergency room.

It's hard to say for sure what triggered it, but I suspect that the combination of starting college and the holiday season may have contributed to my reckless behavior. I was hospitalized on January 23rd, 1996. Again....

The doctor's notes from my hospital stay, *'Patient admitted due to being very active and energetic and somewhat agitated at times. Her sleeping has diminished dramatically, and her appetite has become poor. She developed a great deal of religiosity. She has some push of speech and flight of ideas. An altercation occurred with her father. Father states, "Can't handle being around her. Her mood is mild to moderate euphoria, bordering on a flight of ideas. She has been bizarrely communicating with people in "sign languages." '*

That was it; I was in the hospital again. I didn't understand why. I didn't want their medications; the medications they put me on in the past gave me horrible side effects. The experiences I had here were dreadful; why would I want to comply? I was on a 72-hour hold for three days and released on January 25th.

Following the incident, my relationship with Scott came to an end. While I was the one who initiated the breakup, I can't seem to remember the exact reason behind it. It was an arduous period for me, and I found myself struggling to cope with the aftermath of the incident.

There are moments in my life that I wish I could have handled differently. However, due to my mental state at the time, I found it difficult to control my actions and words. I strongly believe that Scott's family are wonderful people who deserve nothing but the best treatment. I pray that they continue to be blessed.

College year two

My second year of college proved to be a refreshing change. I was taking courses that genuinely intrigued me, and I also managed to make some new friends. Among these was a tall, attractive law enforcement student who caught my eye. We clicked instantly and began talking and getting to know each other better.

One day, he asked me out on a date, and since I found him charming and interesting, I accepted his invitation. It felt good to move on from my past and explore new possibilities. Despite the challenges I had recently faced, I knew that life still had much to offer.

The law enforcement student asked me to meet up at the college. He greeted me warmly and asked how my day had been. He then suggested that we go out for dinner.

We hopped in his car and made our way to a restaurant in Hibbing. The place was cozy and welcoming, with warm lighting and soft music playing in the background. We settled into our seats and perused the menu, chatting amicably about our interests and hobbies.

I ordered fried chicken with a salad for dinner, and he had a hamburger and fries. The food was exquisite, and we savored every bite, continuing our conversation and learning more about each other.

After dinner, he suggested we catch a movie at the local theater. We decided to watch a comedy movie since it's fun to laugh. The film ended around 9:30 pm, and I left the theater feeling uplifted and cheerful. He asked if we could stop by his apartment before he took me back to my car. He said he needed to grab a few things and invited me inside. I agreed to follow him into his apartment. He asked me to sit down while he grabbed his warmer jacket. He then came up next to me, sitting down beside me. His hand brushed against my cheek as if to kiss me. I leaned away, showing reluctance. He squinted his eyes at me as if disgusted.

He said, *"Come on, kiss me."*

I said, *"I want to go."*

He pushed me down, pinning my arms and shoulders in place, and forced himself on me. In the horror that followed, my mind blocked details. The handsome law enforcement student turned into a monster. This happened in the fall of '96 when I was 19, making my second year of college seem bleak.

"Through the storm of bad decisions and horrible experiences, I still knew Jesus loved me through it all. He was always there, no matter what."

Be pleased, oh Lord, to deliver me; hurry, Oh Lord, to help me. - Psalm 40:13

Chapter 4

Rollercoaster Ride

Crazy

Not much after the horrific event, I experienced a significant shift in my personality and behavior. I was unaware of this change, but my family noticed I was acting differently. I was saying odd things and not sleeping well, which clearly indicated something was wrong. My family was concerned that if left unaddressed, this state of mind could lead to something unpleasant happening to me.

I used to drive an off-white '82 Mercury Cougar with a reddish roof. It was a long, boat-like car, and I loved driving it all over to the point of oblivion. I drove it recklessly, thinking that I was having fun. I met a girl named Katie at college, and we became friends.

One day, I asked her if she had ever been to the top of the world. She was surprised and asked where it was. I told her that I would take her there, and she agreed. We got into my '82 Cougar, and I started talking excitedly about everything under the sun. We took a left turn just past the gas station at the North end of town and started ascending on the red-orange iron ore trail.

The trail was winding and rough, but we kept going until we reached a point where it flattened out and got out of the car. I pointed out different things to Katie, like the college and the scenery around us. However, Katie didn't enjoy it and asked if we could return. I agreed, but instead of driving back slowly, I revved the engine and drove recklessly down the trail, hitting rocks and holes.

I thought it was fun, but Katie started crying and begged me to slow down. I didn't listen and continued driving recklessly, laughing at Katie's fear. We made it back to the bottom without any issues, but Katie was upset and asked me to stop at the gas station. She got out of the car and said she would find another ride. Katie didn't talk to me after that.

I continued to spiral out of control, not coming home. I would drive recklessly all over the Iron Range.

I barely slept and would ramble on about nonsensical things.

I was irritable, irrational, and obnoxious. Everything made sense to me in my world, but my actions didn't make sense to those around me.

My thoughts would race and run, never-ending ideas and goals.

I would talk to anyone around me, and my filter was shut off. I hung out with people I didn't know and even slept with random guys.

I felt an immense sense of power coursing through my veins. I was convinced that I was invincible and could do things better than anyone I met.

Apparently, this *"episode"* was much worse than the past couple of episodes I had in high school, and I was out of control. I NEVER recognized the symptoms; I felt normal.

I drove to the college as usual, noticed Scott at a distance, and yelled, *"Hey Scott, come here!"* In my peripheral vision, I saw my mom pull up near me. My bravado was shattered as I caught sight of a police officer walking towards me.

As I was about to take off running, my mom called out to me, her voice stern yet loving. *"Vicky, you have to go,"* she said, her eyes filled with concern. Standing at a distance, Scott watched me with a reassuring gaze, silently communicating that everything would be alright. Despite my anxiety, I felt a sense of comfort in his presence, knowing that he would always be there for me.

Diagnosed

I found myself back in the hospital once again in October 1996. It's on the same floor but with a new security setup. The door is now locked and requires a nurse to unlock it, leaving me feeling confined and restricted. While hospitalized, my mind played tricks on me, causing me to do strange things like moving the deck of cards around in the common area, thinking it would somehow alter my reality. The TV, once a source of entertainment, became

unbearable as I felt like the voices were speaking directly to me, causing me to avoid the common area altogether. It was a strange and isolating experience, and I found myself feeling trapped in my own mind.

Dr. Leroy examined me daily. He decided to wipe my medication list clean and start with a clean slate. I'll never forget that day he said, *"I believe you have bipolar, bipolar type I. I, too, am bipolar. We'll try 1200mg of Lithium and 1500mg of Depakote."* Well, now I have a name for all my madness, bipolar.

I was locked up in the hospital for weeks, no fresh air. Moments turned into hours, hours into days; I felt ashamed, alone, afraid, and now depressed. I asked Dr. Leroy if I could go home. He replied, *"No, we need to let your body adjust to the medication, Lithium particularly."*

My parents made sure to visit me as often as possible despite the short visiting hours. One particular day, while my parents were there, my dad struck up a conversation with a Native American man who was also a patient in the hospital. As they talked, it quickly became apparent that they shared a deep passion for the great outdoors. They discussed their favorite trapping locations and fishing spots and had a similar sense of humor. Their conversation was animated, and I could see they quickly bonded over their shared interests. As my parents prepared to leave, my dad exchanged phone numbers with his new friend, promising to keep in touch and make plans for future outdoor adventures. Dr. Leroy allowed me to go on a day pass to spend time with my family for my niece's school event. I was so thankful to be leaving for the day and really hoped never to return to that dreadful place.

Grief

After the beautiful day with my family, I figured it wouldn't be much longer before I would return home, go to college, and live normally. No. Instead, I was escorted by a nurse down a hallway through the locked door to a white room. To my right was a judge dressed in a typical black robe. To my left, my parents were seated and watching me as I entered the room.

The judge told me to sit down; I don't recall much after that except something about me not going home. I looked at my mom for answers, and tears streamed down her face. *"I can't go home?"* I whispered. Mom shook her head sympathetically, saying, *"Sorry."*

Well, I did get to leave the hospital but not go home. No, I had to live in an assisted living in Chisholm. It was here they managed my medications, fed me my meals, and offered *'help.'* As I longed to return to my usual self and live an everyday life, a social worker from the county appeared at my *'new home.'* She greeted me warmly and introduced herself as my appointed worker to assist me. Standing tall with short blonde hair, she had a pleasant demeanor. At first, I declined her aid, thinking I didn't need it.

However, she handed me some forms I had to complete for the state. It was a few forms, but I was preoccupied with the desire to get back to my old self.

Reckless

Despite living in an assisted living facility, I yearned for a bit of adventure. So, I often drove my beloved 1982 Cougar around the area, exploring new roads and meeting new people. However, one fateful night, as I was driving on the East side of Hibbing, I found myself inexplicably drawn to a trail. Perhaps the sense of danger drew me in, or maybe I just needed to feel alive again. Whatever the reason, I found myself driving along the trail, lost in my thoughts. Thoughts that most wouldn't have. But before I knew it, my car got stuck in muddy terrain.

It was pitch dark outside, and I was all alone. So, I decided to brave the woods and set out on foot, determined to find my way back to town. After a long and uncertain trek, I finally returned to the road and into town. I called my parents, who were upset. But when they arrived at the scene, I was mortified to see that someone I knew had come to tow my car out of the mud. To make matters worse, my trusty Cougar was so severely damaged it was totaled.

My parents brought me back to the assisted living, hoping I would rest.

Apparently, I was having another manic episode just a month after the last, even though I was taking my medications. Reports were made that I was acting strange and barely sleeping. I wandered around Chisholm at night when it was freezing out. I recall walking on the trail next to Long year Lake. I'm sure I was overly exhausted from not sleeping.

While strolling along the trail, I was drawn to the lush grass by the lake, deeming it ideal for a leisurely walk. To my dismay, I soon discovered it was the lake itself, teeming with lily pads and thick weeds. Frantically, I struggled back to shore, trapped by the entangling vegetation. The November chill permeated the air, and the cold water bit into my skin as I fought my way free. With the eerie silence of 3:00 am enveloping me, I found myself utterly alone.

Seeking refuge from the biting cold, I stumbled upon an unlocked car parked nearby, hoping to find warmth within its confines. Disheartened by the lack of respite, I ventured towards the attached garage of a nearby house, its door left unlocked. Driven by a manic impulse, I resorted to desperate measures, smashing a spare oven in a misguided attempt to generate heat.

My actions stirred the owner from sleep, and confronted me in the garage. Overwhelmed by embarrassment, I offered a false name when questioned. Despite his offer of assistance, shame consumed me, compelling me to request to be dropped off a block away from my parents' home. The arrival of the police marked the culmination of my tumultuous night, culminating in yet another hospitalization and a 72-hour hold in the psychiatric ward.

Depression

After these extreme episodes, totaling my car, not having any close friends, and my family not being able to handle how I was, I felt stuck, hurt, and alone. I felt I would never leave the assisted living. I thought I would end up like my relatives, who are mentally ill and appear to be stuck that way. I thought I was never going to change and be this crazy, unliked person for the rest of my life.

My parents, overwhelmed by my erratic behavior, struggled to comprehend the turmoil within me. I never intended to exhibit such distressing conduct; all I longed for was to blend in and be perceived as *"normal"* like my peers. However, faced with their own bewilderment, my parents reluctantly sought assistance from the county. While I harbor no ill will towards them, the intervention shattered me deeply.

Suddenly, thrust into the care of social workers and residing in unfamiliar surroundings, I grappled with an overwhelming sense of isolation and despair. The profound loneliness that engulfed me felt insurmountable, leaving me to confront the depths of my anguish with no solace in sight.

Day in and day out, I would *'live'* in assisted living. I was so depressed I barely ate; I mainly slept. I'd stay in bed while I read my bible. I cried and prayed that the Lord would help and deliver me from my despair. I can still vividly remember the room I had at the assisted living facility. The walls were covered in old wood

paneling, and the bed was so uncomfortable that it squeaked every time I moved. The room itself was incredibly small, reminiscent of a dingy motel room. The bathroom was furnished with dark brown and orange decor that seemed to be from the 1960s, and it had a similarly dingy and outdated vibe to it. I can still see myself sitting up in bed, crying while reading the Bible - I spent a lot of time doing that during my stay there.

Hope

In November 1997, my sister extended an invitation to join her and our other sister, Rose, at a church event in Duluth, MN. Despite my initial hesitations, I decided to accept. The event centered around a band performing worship songs while the congregation sang praises to the Lord. Seated between my sisters in the front row, I couldn't find the will to join in the singing.

Suddenly, the worship leader paused, his words cutting through the solemnity of the moment. *"The Lord wants those struggling to be free,"* he declared. *"Someone here has been dealing with depression. Get up and come to the altar and receive from the Lord."*

Tears welled in my eyes as I glanced at my sisters. Though the weight of my struggles felt insurmountable, Rose and Jen offered their support, helping me to my feet.

As I went to the front, joining others in praise, an inexplicable wave of emotion swept over me. Though no one laid hands on me or uttered a prayer, as I expressed gratitude to Jesus, the heaviness of depression lifted instantaneously. A profound sense of joy enveloped me in its place, igniting laughter and disbelief within my soul. God had answered my prayers, granting me the freedom I had long yearned for.

That transformative night in Duluth marked a pivotal turning point in my journey, etching itself into the fabric of my being as one of my most cherished and unforgettable life experiences. In the wake of this spiritual awakening, my parents noticed a profound change within me, extending an invitation to return home and start anew.

Feeling Normal

I started working at a group home where I assisted adults with developmental disabilities. The job was highly fulfilling, and I was glad I was able to help them lead a better life. I spent most of my day tending to the needs of these adults, and I was happy to see them smile with every small accomplishment they made.

I found solace in tending to our beloved dogs in my leisure hours. Our walks in the park were a delightful departure from the mundane, offering a refreshing respite from the daily grind.

Equally important was my commitment to attending church, a cornerstone of my life. In its embrace, I discovered a profound sense of belonging and tranquility. The serenity within its walls was unmatched, providing a sanctuary from the world's chaos outside.

I found fulfillment in balancing my professional endeavors and the meaningful pursuits that enriched my life beyond the confines of work.

A bump in the road

Despite understanding the criticality of adhering to my medication regimen, I began to feel overly self-assured about my well-being and discontinued taking my medications as prescribed. Convinced of my stability, I rationalized that I no longer needed the medication. Unfortunately, I failed to recognize the jeopardy I was placing my mental health in by neglecting this essential aspect of my treatment.

In October 1998, my miscalculation led to yet another hospitalization. Concerned for my well-being, my parents sought assistance from the authorities, resulting in police escorting me back to the psychiatric ward. The reports outlined symptoms of agitation, an inability to cooperate, rapid speech, and evidence of racing thoughts, culminating in another 72-hour hold for evaluation and treatment.

The medications, The mania

Since 1992, I've been prescribed a myriad of medications, each accompanied by its own set of distressing side effects. Among the medications I've taken between 1992 and 1998 are Navan 10mg tid, Cogentin 2mg qd, Klonopin 1.5mg qd, Tegretol 200mg qid, Depakote 250mg qid, Trilafon 4mg qd, Haldol 7.5mg qd, Lithium 300mg qid, and Ativan 2mg qd. Despite the array of medications, none seemed to prevent the onset of manic episodes.

My care team, along with my family, embarked on a quest to decipher the triggers behind each manic episode. It became apparent that my manic episodes often coincided with the onset of my menstrual cycle or during colder seasons. Despite our efforts, nothing seemed to stave off the recurrence of mania. Additionally, the depressive episodes that followed were equally debilitating, compounding the challenges I faced.

I found myself trapped in a relentless cycle, where progress was elusive, and setbacks were inevitable. Despite having stable employment, a reliable vehicle, and a circle of friends, the tumult of bipolar disorder often left wreckage in its wake. I would succumb to impulsive shopping sprees, splurging on extravagant items, only to give them away shortly after that.

The lack of sleep exacerbated the chaos in my life, reaching a point where I reportedly endured five sleepless nights during one manic episode. The hospital staff bore witness to my incessant chatter, heightened agitation, bouts of yelling, and vivid hallucinations. Over time, I received varying diagnoses, including schizophrenia, and acute psychosis, until the definitive diagnosis of bipolar type 1 was reached

Status Quo

In the years that followed, I appeared stable in my mental health. I was able to maintain a somewhat normal life for some time. I had the opportunity to volunteer at a Christian camp nestled in the beautiful Western Minnesota region. I met some of the most amazing people who significantly shaped my life during my time there. The experience also helped me grow in my faith and allowed me to impact the young campers' lives positively.

I did meet a guy who was also volunteering at the camp. We started dating, why, I don't know. I wasn't even attracted to him. I didn't like his personality either. He was manipulative, and he drank a ton.

After wrapping up my volunteer stint at the camp, I wanted to change scenery away from Chisholm. Fortunately, my sister Rose presented an enticing opportunity: to stay with her in Bloomington and care for her two children while she balanced school and work commitments. Eagerly, I embraced the chance and found immense joy in nurturing my adorable niece, Sarah, and infant nephew, Adel. I secured a temporary job alongside my caregiving responsibilities, adding a fulfilling dimension to my days.

During my time living with my sister, I ended the relationship with the drunk; he wasn't worth my time. I'm thankful I was emotionally strong enough to end it with him.

Despite having parted ways with Scott months earlier, lingering feelings persisted. Our occasional phone conversations kept the connection alive, and serendipitously, he found himself in the area visiting his brother one day. Seizing the opportunity, I invited him to my sister's place, where we spent the day together. Immersed in each other's company, the past seemed to dissolve, and our bond reignited effortlessly. The apartment complex had a pool, so we swam and hung out, and it was like we had never broken up. We relished spending time together, and soon after, we got back together officially.

I decided to move back home to Chisholm to be close to Scott. It was a big decision, but I knew it was right. I was excited to start a new chapter in my life with the person I loved, and I knew that things would work out for the best.

"I clung to the hope of my salvation in Jesus.

He was my shelter, my strong shield in my despair."

Indeed, God is my salvation; I will trust and not be afraid. The Lord, the Lord himself, is my strength and my song; he has become my salvation. - Isaiah 12:2

Chapter 5

My Heritage

I want to share and go back in time to where it all started: the Iron Range—a place where my family's generations hail from.

The Iron Range

The place that has laid the foundation of my family's legacy is the Iron Range. It is situated in Northeastern Minnesota and is known for its vast iron ore deposits, which have been mined for over a century. The region is also home to dense forests of towering pines that were once used to fuel the iron smelters. The Iron Range is where my family's roots lie and where many of my ancestors have worked in the mines and lived their lives.

The Iron Range is breathtaking and holds a special place in my heart. My parents, Kenneth Anthony Rosc and Anita Hope (Chase) Rosc, hail from the Iron Range. My dad was born and raised in Chisholm, while my mom was from Hibbing.

The Iron Range boasts a prominent role in the United States steel production, owing to its abundant iron ore deposits. Among its remarkable features, the Hull Rust Mine, dubbed the Grand Canyon of the North, stands out as the world's largest open-pit iron ore mine. Serving as a poignant symbol of the region's mining legacy, it beckons visitors to witness the immense scale of human endeavor involved in ore extraction. Exploring its depths offers a captivating glimpse into the area's rich history. Moreover, the old mining pits, now transformed into serene aqua-blue reservoirs, add to the area's allure, creating a truly mesmerizing spectacle.

Driving through the Iron Range, life slows down compared to other regions of Minnesota. The people of the Iron Range are tough, hardworking folks. They love spending time outdoors and engaging in activities such as fishing, hunting, snowmobiling, and ATV riding. The numerous lakes offer plenty of opportunities for swimming, boating, fishing, and other water-based activities. The region is also known for its delicious food, including Slovenian potica, Italian porchetta, and "miners" pasties, among other culinary delights.

The Iron Range is a remarkable region that is both small and mighty. The region is characterized by the impenetrable coldness and the unyielding strength of the iron ore that is mined from its depths. Once, I stumbled upon a comment online that drew a comparison between the Iron Range and a less gritty Appalachia, and the comparison is quite fitting. The people who inhabit this region are known for their hard work, resilience, and unflinching determination in the face of adversity. They are also people who know how to enjoy the simplicities of life and have a good time. The Iron Range is a truly unique and special place that embodies the spirit of the people who call it home.

Family story

My mom, during her younger days, was a reserved and modest individual. She spent her childhood spending time with her sisters. Her house was originally in North Hibbing, which was famously known as the *'town that moved.'* The house where she lived was relocated to East Hibbing due to the expansion of the mine, and consequently, a large part of North Hibbing was mined.

When my mom was only 15 years old, my grandpa Carlos passed away. It was a profound loss, but sadly, I don't think my mom ever had the chance to mourn his death properly. She confided in me that she was just a child herself and felt somewhat numb during that difficult time. With Grandpa gone, Grandma Zora was left to care for herself and the children single-handedly.

Mom recounted how Grandma Zora, despite her own grief, worked tirelessly to provide for the family. She sewed clothes for them, and they relied on hand-me-downs to make ends meet. However, Grandpa's passing took a heavy toll on Grandma Zora. She fell into a deep depression, one that she never fully emerged from. It was a clinical depression that gripped her tightly, casting a shadow over the family's life.

My mom's relationship with her sisters was something extraordinary. She had an aura of intelligence about her that was undeniable, yet she remained incredibly modest. Her intellect was indeed one of her most vital attributes. Although she was often reserved and introverted around others, she had a heart of gold and cared deeply for others. Reading was a passion of hers that she indulged in at every opportunity. Whether she was relaxing in her free time, taking a break while using the restroom, or enjoying a snack, she always had a book in hand. Late at night, she would savor the tartness of Granny Smith apples. I believe my mom struggled with her self-esteem and self-worth. She loved talking to her friends on the phone and had a particular fondness for animals, especially horses. Unfortunately, her allergies prevented her from getting too close to them, but that didn't stop her from admiring their beauty from afar. All in all, my mom is remarkable.

When my mom turned 21, she and my grandma, Zora, ventured to a bar in Chisholm with the intention of finding a date for Grandma. However, fate had other plans in store. As they sat at their table, a charming and handsome young man approached them and asked my mom for a dance. Initially hesitant, she declined his invitation. Yet, Grandma Zora, ever the encourager, nudged her under the table, urging her to seize the opportunity with such a fine-looking gentleman—a man by the name of Ken Rosc.

While I have limited knowledge about Grandma Zora's family history, I have fond memories of attending Thanksgiving gatherings at my mom's cousin's restaurant, Trappers. These reunions provided glimpses into Grandma's family and added to the tapestry of our family connections. What I do know is that my grandpa, Carlos L. Chase, hailed from a lineage with roots tracing back to the Mayflower. It's fascinating to note that a relative, James P. Chase, once served on the Supreme Court during Lincoln's presidency, a fact that I find quite remarkable.

From what my mom has shared, Grandpa Carlos was a jovial and compassionate man who had a knack for making others feel at ease in his presence. He was a devoted father and left behind cherished memories of his warmth and kindness. Though I never had the chance to know him personally, his legacy lives on through the stories and fond recollections shared by my family.

In 1923, my great-grandfather Carlos S. Chase organized a Boy Scout canoe trip as part of the Northern Tier High Adventure, now Charles L. Sommers Wilderness Canoe Base. At the base, my relatives celebrated the 100 anniversary with other individuals in 2023. This is the oldest high-adventure camp in the US. My great-grandfather also planted the red pines with his troop on *'Boy Scout Hill'* in Hibbing.

My mom's family embodied a quiet yet close-knit dynamic, characterized by kindness and humility. Among them, my grandma Zora stood out for her remarkable crafting skills. Proficient in crocheting doilies, quilts, and tablecloths, she often showcased her talents at family gatherings. These gatherings held great significance in our lives, serving as moments to share meals, exchange stories, and revel in laughter. Many of these cherished moments unfolded at Grandma's house, while others took place at my Aunt Shari's residence, where we continued to deepen our familiar bonds amidst the serene backdrop of horseback rides and lakeside relaxation.

On the other side, my dad hailed from the vibrant Rosc family, where music and Catholic traditions held sway. Singing together accompanied by guitar melodies was common in their midst, reflecting their lively spirit and deep-rooted faith. Attending Catholic mass held paramount importance for them.

My dad, an ardent lover of the outdoors, spent years working in the mines, eventually rising to the position of foreman. In the tight-knit community of the Iron Range, mining or related occupations were prevalent among men, reflecting the region's industrial landscape and the livelihoods it offered.

My family has shared stories about my dad from the past, and they paint a picture of a complex man with a rich history. As the eldest of six siblings, he took on the role of protector, especially for his sister. He had a habit of taking the blame for things he didn't do, even when it meant getting into trouble. But while he may have had his share of misdeeds growing up, there was a deep empathy in him that led him to carry other people's burdens as well.

My dad experienced hardship early on in life, but he never talked about it. It's as if he internalized his pain and used humor or anger to mask his true feelings. Still, he had a gift for storytelling that drew people in. Whenever he spoke, the room would fall silent as everyone hung on his every word.

Despite his emotional distance, my dad did his best as a father. He was a flawed man who loved his family but struggled to express it. He drank heavily like many Iron Rangers, often to the point of drunkenness. And while he loved my mom, his passion for the outdoors sometimes took precedence over his responsibilities at home.

In all, my dad was a complex man with a rich and complicated history.

In my family lineage, there's my Slavanian grandfather, Joe, whose parents astonishingly raised thirteen children. Joe was a miner, a prevalent occupation in our region. Despite my young age of five when he passed, I fondly remember his bright red nose and the pocket change he often gifted me.

Then, there's Jenny (Ganina) Marana Rosc, affectionately known as Nanny. A spirited Sicilian, she delighted in cooking delectable meals for anyone who crossed her path. Known for her warm hugs, she wasn't one to shy away from speaking her mind when warranted. Her signature phrase, *"Go pee up a rope,"* was often directed at misbehaving boys, her distinctive knobby index finger emphasizing her point.

Eating Nanny's homemade ravioli became a cherished tradition in our family, especially during Christmas. The anticipation would build until the moment the ravioli was served, and we'd all gather around the table, relishing each flavorful bite with joy and gratitude.

Tradition followed with us partaking in helping make Nanny's ravioli. From the moment we gathered in the kitchen, there was a palpable sense of excitement and anticipation in the air. Everyone had a role to play, whether it was kneading the dough, shaping the pasta, or mixing the filling. Nanny was the true star of the show, with her expert knowledge and skill guiding us through each step of the process. The tradition didn't end there - we also indulged in Nanny's famous fudge, a rich and decadent treat that had become a staple of our family gatherings.

The Rosc clan stands as a captivating and unforgettable assembly of individuals, each brimming with their own distinctive tales and idiosyncrasies—a vibrant and talented bunch indeed. Aunt MaryRose possessed a voice that could rival the finest singers, coupled with a gift for storytelling that held her audience spellbound. Meanwhile, Grandpa Joe's resonant voice reverberated through the Catholic Church, accompanied by other family members' melodious strumming of guitars.

Whenever the clan assembled, it was an occasion to indulge in homemade delights like donuts, cookies, bread, and fudge, all boasting sweetness potent enough to set one's teeth on edge. Laughter permeated the household, ranging from hearty belly laughs to the raucous cackling of hens, with jokes flying and banter flowing freely, ensuring everyone's sides ached from mirth. Amidst promises of Christmas caroling and shared revelry, nothing quite matched the anticipation and joy of Christmas day itself. We'd gather together in spirited rounds of board games such as charades or Pictionary, sparking raucous and exhilarating moments that left everyone buoyed by high spirits and cherished memories.

Parent's marriage

On a particular summer day, June 11th, 1966, the weather alternated between sunshine and rain as my parents exchanged their marriage vows at the Catholic church. Mom, nearly 22 years old, radiated beauty in her white wedding dress, while dad, 27, exuded elegance in his dark suit. Though I was not yet born, I can only imagine the emotions that must have coursed through their veins on that special day. They embarked on their married life by living in an affordable housing apartment situated close to Dad's parents' residence before eventually deciding to purchase a house on the charming Northwest side of Chisholm.

Siblings

Before my arrival, my family had already embraced three incredible individuals. Their names are Roseann Marie, Gregory Kenneth, and Jennifer Jo. Each of them holds a special place in my heart, and their presence has shaped our family in countless ways. Each of them has a unique and interesting story to tell. Rose, the eldest of the three siblings, was born in the 1960s and had a passion for health and helping others, while Greg, the middle child, was born in the late 1960s and has an inquisitive and adventurous personality. Jen, the youngest of the three, was born in the early 1970s and has a love to host and care for others, all very talented as well. Despite their differences, they all shared a strong bond as siblings. They contributed to the rich tapestry of our family history.

1977

The year was marked by several significant events that had a lasting impact on society. The United States witnessed the inauguration of Jimmy Carter as the President of the country while the world mourned the loss of a music icon, Elvis Presley. The entertainment industry was revolutionized with the release of Star Wars Episode IV, which captivated audiences around the globe. The gaming world was transformed with Atari's arrival in the US, which paved the way for the modern video game industry. Additionally, technology took a giant leap forward with the release of Apple II, which marked the beginning of a new era in personal computing.

When my mom was pregnant with me, she had to be hospitalized due to hypertension. My dad was working as a police officer at that time. My aunt stayed with my older siblings and took care of them while my mom was in the hospital. However, during that time, medical technology was not as advanced as today, and doctors couldn't detect every issue during pregnancy. Eventually, my mom went into labor; she was bleeding heavily, and the doctors had to perform an emergency C-section at 12:05 am on April 12th, 1977. Placenta Previa caused heavy bleeding during my mom's labor, which can be fatal for the mother and/or baby. As a result, both my mom and I had to spend a long time in the hospital.

During difficult times in my life, Mom would share how special I was because of the emergency birth. I think she would remind me about it to empathize with me when I was struggling.

I was born with thick black hair, weighing 9lb 10 oz, and my parents named me Vicky Lee Rosc. At the time of my birth, my older brother Greg was 8.5 years old. When he and my other siblings visited me in the hospital, Greg jokingly said that I looked like a monkey due to all the hair on my head. Greg, having a vivid imagination, I can imagine I did resemble a little monkey with my mop of black hair.

My dad worked as a police officer in the year 1977 and also assisted the community. When I was a child, my mom shared with me how my dad bravely fought a massive forest fire when I was a baby. The wildfire broke out in Minog, Wisconsin, on April 30th, 1977, and spread rapidly, and about 1600 people showed up to help contain it. My dad had a heroic attitude, which suited him well to fight the blaze. As it turned out, every volunteer was paid a minimum hourly wage to fight the fire, only $2.30. It is hard to believe that people were paid such a meager amount, which is not enough even to buy a bottle of pop at a gas station nowadays!

Looking back, I felt terrible for my mom. She had three normal births before I was born, then had this emergency c-section where she was cut vertically during the c-section, preventing the muscles in her abdomen from being normal again. She was also overweight for as long as I can remember. Sadly, I sometimes blamed myself for her weight because I thought it was from the c-section.

"I have always enjoyed learning about my family heritage. I love my family regardless of differences or being apart. My parents were key to my foundation in faith in Jesus and a shelter even in their own storms."

Finally, all of you, be like-minded, be sympathetic, love one another, be compassionate and humble. - 1 Peter 3:8

Chapter 6

Childhood

Broken child

When I was so young and innocent, I experienced a terrible event. I was touched and hurt by that man in ways no child should ever experience. My soul was harmed, and my deepest being was impacted by sexual assault.

That horrible experience in my life was blocked out of my memory... Such abuse caused many problems in my later years. While in therapy many years later, I realized how deeply it affected me.

Memories of old

We all cherish memories, though their strength varies from person to person. One vivid memory for me is the day my mom decided it was time to part with my baby blanket, a significant step in my growing up.

As an infant, I had a distinct way of moving—I preferred scooting forward over the typical crawling. This quirk often puzzled my parents, who watched in bemusement. Adding to the intrigue, our family was amidst a home renovation project, leaving me to explore amidst the construction chaos. Our house, with its history dating back to 1911, was engulfed in dust from the demolition work. I roamed through the debris, leaving trails in my wake.

Reflecting on those days, I can't help but chuckle at the sight I must have presented—scooting around amidst the chaos and dust, unfazed by the commotion. However, the thought of the dust possibly containing lead paint still sends shivers down my spine.

My sister Jennifer shared with me that our parents fought viscously during the remodel. My older siblings would go to friends' houses or relatives. At the same time, I was left in the dust of the remodel, listening to my parents' crazy behavior. Granted, I don't remember all of this, but I'm sure it affected me.

After the remodel was completed, I was engrossed in playing with my toys, as any young child would, when suddenly, the atmosphere in our home changed. My dad's booming voice filled the air, accompanied by heated arguments between him and my mom emanating from their bedroom. The sound of my mom being thrashed around while her cries pierced through the chaos. My dad's struggles with alcohol had turned him into a volatile presence in our household, and this evening was no exception.

As a frightened four-year-old, I instinctively sought solace in the comfort of an oversized pillow lying nearby. Clutching it tightly, tears welled up in my eyes as I lay there, motionless, trying to block out the turmoil unfolding around me.

After the storm subsided, my dad approached me, and his demeanor softened. Sitting beside me on the floor, he gently stroked my hair and whispered reassuring words. But his tone quickly shifted as he directed blame towards my mom, who stood in the doorway with tears streaming down her face. *"Look what you've done, you made her cry!"* he admonished sternly.

Even now, this memory remains vivid in my mind, a poignant reminder of the tumultuous dynamics within my childhood home.

As soon as my parents began to argue, my siblings knew it was time to leave the house. They would hold hands and run outside, seeking refuge in the safety of our neighbor's home or walk around the neighborhood. It was not uncommon for my parents' arguments to escalate into full-blown fights, and we often experienced the full brunt of their anger and frustration. Through it all, my siblings together, finding solace in each other's company and the brief moments of peace they could steal away from the chaos. I was much younger than my siblings; I was left with my parents during their chaotic fights. I feel bad for my siblings for the trauma they experienced from my parents. I don't remember, or I didn't see as much chaos from my parents since I was so much younger when they fought.

Even though I don't remember much of the physical fights, I am sure what I witnessed took a toll on my developing mind.

What I witnessed of how my parents acted in their relationship affected how I acted in my own relationships. Although I wasn't co-dependent like my mom, I still struggled with controlling my emotions. This is something that I continue to struggle with to this day.

My dad was an alcoholic who was saved by God's grace when I was about four years old. He quit drinking and smoking cold turkey, but his alcoholic rage seethed on towards my mom at times when he would yell, but he never hit her again.

I am grateful that my parents' lives changed after they developed a relationship with the Lord. Although they still had many struggles, they remained steadfast and faithful in their faith. I witnessed my mom reading the Bible fervently in the kitchen, living room, and even the bathroom. My dad also spent time reading the word, mainly early in the morning, before anyone else woke up. I strongly believe that their changed lives and fervent prayers had a positive impact on my own life.

Cabin

Nestled among the towering pine trees, our cabin stood proudly, with a soft, sandy beach stretching along the tranquil shore of Scooty Lake. My parents worked hard to keep the beach clear of weeds. It was a favorite place for my older siblings, Roseann, Greg, and Jennifer, who would spend hours playing on a gigantic intertube that was probably made from a tire off a large dump truck from the Iron Ore mines. Despite the terrible mosquitoes, we all loved being at the cabin, surrounded by the intoxicating scent of the deep woods that enveloped us, reminding us that we were far away from the city. Although I was just a young child at the time, the memories of our time at the cabin with my siblings are still etched in my mind.

As a young kid, I sat beside my mom in our green station wagon with brown strips along the side. Rose and her best friend were in the back seat heading to our old cabin. Mom shared how a truck with a camper was driving in the center of the dirt road, causing her to swerve and dodge the camper trailer. As she was swerving and slamming on the brakes, I flew forward, hitting my head on the dashboard. She said she put her arm in front of me, trying to prevent the blow, but I still hit it hard with my head, giving me a black eye. Poor Rose, 13 at the time, got her face scraped up from branches because the window was open. Oh, the days of no seat belts, kids riding shotgun,' no car seats, and big station wagons.

Our cabin could have been more enjoyable as it was old and smelled musty. It was more like a dingy trailer house. My older siblings discovered baby chipmunks in one of the bunk beds. While playing on the innertube, Greg accidentally cut his arm.

One sunny July day when I was four at our ol' cabin, I was in an orange and blue plastic floating tube in the shallow water— somehow, I flipped upside down. I recall seeing the beams of sunshine dancing on the sand while I was stuck underwater. Rose was floating on a floating device, basking in the sun further out. She swam frantically, saving me from my drowning demise. I feared water, especially when I couldn't see the bottom. Learning to swim took me a while; I didn't know how to swim until 7th grade.

Me at the cabin with my floating tube

Personalities and Traits

As the second youngest sibling in my family, I always looked up to my older siblings, Rose, Greg, and Jen, who were significantly older than me. Each of them had unique qualities that I admired. Rose had a bright and kind demeanor, which made her approachable and likable. Greg, on the other hand, had a natural talent for art and music that always amazed me. Jen, meanwhile, had a beautiful singing voice that I could listen to all day.

Apart from their personal qualities, I also shared some of Greg's interests in rock and coin collecting, which I found fascinating. I would often tag along with him whenever he went out to collect them. Jen, on the other hand, played volleyball, and I was always eager to join in and play with her.

Despite my admiration for my older siblings, I must admit that I could be an annoying little sister at times. My brother Greg once shared a funny story about how my mom asked him to come and get me while I was playing when I was about three years old. When he picked me up, I bit him really hard on the nose, which left a lasting impression on both of us.

Rose writes beautiful poems and has such a tender heart. Being the eldest, she felt she should look after her siblings. She spent much of her teenage years babysitting me. After all, she is ten years my senior!

I ruined Jen's Barbie dolls. Instead of playing with them, I popped the legs and headed off. I wasn't much into playing with dolls. Jen would get so mad at me because I played with her toys. We were a little closer in age, six and a half years apart.

One event I will never forget is when our neighbor needed help putting together a metal shed. My family was assisting, and I was running around barefoot. I was around five years old when my toe was sliced by the edge of the shed panel, and it started bleeding profusely. Greg swooped me up in his arms and gingerly carried me home to get my toe bandaged by my mom.

Learning & Art

During my childhood, I saw myself as normal. However, I faced some challenges while learning essential skills. For instance, it took me quite some time to master the art of tying my shoes, which I eventually managed to do at the age of seven. Similarly, riding a bike was another hurdle that I had to overcome, and it was when I turned ten that I finally succeeded. Additionally, I had some difficulties with reading and math, which led to me being placed in a class meant for slow readers.

I recall a vicious elementary teacher. I couldn't understand greater and lesser than in math. She yelled at me from the front of the classroom, *"Come up here and write it on the board!"* I gulped and slowly walked to the front of the class. I couldn't get it, I didn't understand. She grabbed my ear, pulled it up, and marched me out of the class. That's all I recall from that memory. She made me sit in the hallway until the end of class.

For the most part, childhood was pleasant for me. I spent most of the time with my friends playing four squares, hide and seek, LEGOS, building forts, and searching for night crawlers for fishing. I also rode my bike to the nearby store for candy and to the Chisholm rec for some activities. We had a lot of fun doing everything we could as kids. I also spent considerable time fishing and camping with my dad and groups of people from church. Those were some of my fondest memories ever.

Despite spending most of my time with friends, I had a habit of daydreaming about random things or spending hours drawing with colored pencils. I remember during recess in 3rd grade, while the other kids were playing on the playground, I lay on my stomach drawing the fire hydrant. I loved to draw and still do today. I used to look at pictures of birds and animals from the school library books and draw them the best I could. My 3rd-grade teacher was surprised when he saw a couple of pictures I drew, one of a belted kingfisher and the other of a mountain lion. He didn't believe me when I told him I drew them.

As an individual with a deep passion for art and creativity, I find immense fulfillment in expressing myself through various forms of artistic expression. Despite grappling with certain challenges in my academic journey, such as my tendency to daydream or struggle to fully grasp certain concepts, I feel fortunate to be thriving today. Being able to channel my creativity into my work has allowed me to discover greater meaning and purpose in my life, and I am truly grateful for the opportunity to pursue my passions and share them with the world.

Camping

As the summer season kicked off and came to a close with a bang, my dad, his friends, and us kids eagerly anticipated our camping trips in northeastern Minnesota. Despite the unpredictable weather, especially over Memorial Day weekend, we always looked forward to these adventures. One constant companion on our trips was Mike, a friend of my dad's, who knew the area like the back of his hand. With his knowledge of the lakes and hidden fishing spots, our camping experiences were always unforgettable.

Our favorite spot was Namakan Lake, nestled on the border of Minnesota and Ontario. To get there, we would dock at Nelson's Resort on Crane Lake, navigate through the channels to Sand Point Lake, and finally arrive at Namakan Lake. While we preferred camping on My Island, we didn't mind settling for Your Island if our preferred sites were taken. As kids, we amused ourselves by teasing each other about whose island it really was, making the experience all the more enjoyable.

On our last camping trip, both My Island and Your Island were already occupied, so we ended up on Blind Pig Island. Despite its seemingly odd name, it was a hidden gem. We stumbled upon a serene bay, sheltered from the wind, which was perfect for swimming. The sandy beach beckoned us to its shores, offering a delightful relaxing spot.

The highlight of our trip came when Mike's daughter caught a giant bass using a fishing net—a moment we all cherished and reminisced about long after the trip ended.

One of the most memorable moments of our camping trips was when my dad and I were fishing, and I fell asleep with my line in the water. Suddenly, I heard my dad say, *"Vicky, reel it in; you caught a fish!"* I was thrilled to have caught my biggest walleye!

As kids, we loved searching for arrowheads and remarkable rocks on the sandy shorelines. We also enjoyed stopping at the store in Canada, where an old lady managed the rustic place. We would get mesmerizing candy and watch the rocks and arrowheads pivot on the glass case display.

Camping on Namakan Lake with my childhood best friend, Missy, was one of my fondest memories. We created many unforgettable memories that will always hold a special place in my heart.

Missy

As a young child, my mom required a caregiver to look after me as she worked. Fortunately, our neighbor had a daughter who was only a couple of months older than me, and the neighbor began taking care of me when I was just two and a half years old. Initially, we were merely two infants playing together, but we became the best of friends over time. We were inseparable and shared everything.

Our sleepovers were always the highlight of our time together. We'd stay up late into the night, giggling and chatting while watching movies until we eventually drifted off to sleep. The fun seemed endless, and we never wanted it to stop. Family gatherings were another favorite, filled with games, laughter, and delicious food.

When the weather was nice, we eagerly joined our families for camping and fishing trips. Days were spent exploring the woods, swimming in the lake, and gathering around the campfire at night, roasting marshmallows. We also enjoyed simpler pleasures like riding bikes around the neighborhood, playing with toys, building Legos, and engaging in card games. Our backyard became a haven for creativity as we constructed homemade tents from every spare blanket in the house, much to my mom's chagrin when she had to wash them afterward.

Missy and I shared an unbreakable bond, and our friendship grew stronger each year. Together, we created countless cherished memories that I'll always hold dear. Our childhood friendship will forever remain a precious part of my life.

Missy and I have a plethora of memories we could share. I recall one that is so silly but true. Missy and I dared each other to see who could stick our Play-Doh up our noses the farthest. She can tell the story better. I think we were five years old at the time. Well, my blue Play-Doh fit nicely in my right nostril, and being competitive, I wanted to beat her. I did, but it got stuck in my nose!

We ran into the house to get help from my mom. However, she was too busy talking on the phone and kept ignoring me. I kept grabbing her leg, saying, *"Ma, ma, help, look."* She ignored me for a while but finally looked at me with a surprised expression. She took her tweezers and removed the Play-Doh from my nose, piece by piece.

Trauma - mental illness

I don't recall how old I was, but I was babysat by my relative periodically when my mom worked. I believe my mom went back to work after I was born. Having four children, I'm sure, bore a financial burden on my parents. My relative was quiet. She also had a mental illness; I believe she might have had a schizoaffective disorder. I needed a shower, and my relative required me to help me since I was very young, maybe 5. I recall getting into the shower, and she turned the water on.

I stood facing the back of the shower while she ran the water from the faucet. She turned the shower on, and I felt the scalding hot water piercing my skin. I started to cry out for her to turn it off; by this time, I was pinned up against the back wall, trying to get away from the water. She just laughed and laughed while the water continued to burn my skin. (I don't remember what happened next. I don't think this was intentional, but it sure traumatized me) Another time she was babysitting me, I lost my boot while playing in the snow. I couldn't get it back out of the snow and caved in from my boot. I gingerly walked back into the house, asking her to help me. She just scoffingly laughed, telling me to get it myself. I was so young, yet I recall these incidents.

My relative may have been mentally ill, but I still cared for her and loved her dearly. Dealing with mental illness myself helped me understand. I watched my mom care for and love her unconditionally. I, too, wanted to, just as my mom had.

Family Gatherings

As summertime approached, I eagerly anticipated our annual trip to my uncle's cabin, nestled on the picturesque South Sturgeon Lake. The cabin was a haven of relaxation, delicious homemade treats, and a homemade raft that we kids would jump from, while Nanny, always the mother-hen, would keep a watchful eye and yell, *"Come closer to shore; you're too far out!"*

My uncle had generously enhanced the cabin's amenities by adding a basketball court and a sauna, which added to the enjoyment of our stay. We, kids eagerly anticipated the days filled with swimming and playing, while Dad would take us out in his boat to fish for crappie and walley locating prime fishing spots. We often ventured out to explore the interconnected five-lake chain that included South Sturgeon, navigating through the lengthy channel to Little Sturgeon, Side Lake, Sturgeon Lake, and West Sturgeon.

Our family tradition was to dine together at Bimbo's restaurant on Side Lake. This location had become synonymous with our family reunions. It was a time for us to catch up, reminisce, and create new memories. However, after Nanny passed away in 1997, our family gatherings became infrequent, and the glue that held our Rosc family together was no longer with us. Despite this, my fond memories of our cherished times at the cabin continue to live on.

During my childhood, the holidays and summers were always filled with excitement and anticipation, particularly when we planned visits to my mom's sister, Shari's place. It offered a peaceful contrast to the lively Rosc family gatherings. Initially, I wasn't enthusiastic about spending time with my aunts and other relatives, but as I grew older, I came to appreciate their company and the sense of calm they brought. Today, I treasure our bond and eagerly anticipate seeing them more than any other relatives.

My love for horses began at a young age, thanks to my aunt Alex and cousin Staci. I enjoyed riding horses and learning from their expertise whenever we visited them. The serene atmosphere surrounding their homes was always a highlight for me. I especially cherished our trips to Shari's place on Harriet Lake, where we'd swim, canoe, and explore the stunning scenery. Visiting my Aunt Alex's home in Southeast Minnesota was equally delightful, offering opportunities to spend time outdoors and connect with various animals. These experiences made my childhood truly memorable.

Mom & Dad

Dad never resorted to punishment during my childhood; that was always Mom's domain. Instead, he wielded a powerful gaze that could command immediate compliance. Whenever he shot me "the look," with his wide eyes and intense hazel stare, I knew to fall in line right away. Sometimes, he'd even point, reinforcing his silent directive.

Mom, on the other hand, was the enforcer of discipline. Her threats of *"Knock it off, I'm getting the brush!"* would send us kids scurrying through the house to avoid her wrath. Looking back, it's amusing to recall those moments, though they weren't quite so funny at the time. But the mental image of Mom chasing us still brings a smile to my face.

However, there were times when her discipline crossed the line into a painful territory, like when I refused to eat my salad at around six years old. *"Eat your salad; it's good for you!"* she insisted, but I just couldn't stomach it. *"No, gross!"* I protested. That's when Mom snapped, declaring, *"That's it, you're getting a spanking!"*

She grabbed my arm and dragged me from my chair, through the living room, and into her bedroom. There, she pulled me over her lap, seated in her chair, and proceeded to administer a series of hard spankings, pulling down my pants in the process. While I'm sure her emotions were fueled by various factors, including frustrations with my dad or siblings, at that moment, all I felt was the intense sting of her punishment. It's a memory that remains vivid in my mind to this day.

My mom's love for us kids ran deep, but like any mom, she had her moments of moodiness, especially considering she had to contend with my dad's dry, drunk behavior. Nevertheless, she remained an excellent listener, always ready to lend an ear to our woes. Whether it was offering advice, praying with us, or simply providing comforting hugs, she was there for us through thick and thin, a constant pillar of support throughout my adulthood.

One of Mom's favorite summertime activities was berry picking. As soon as the pink wild roses began to bloom, she'd be out in the fields gathering wild strawberries. Despite their small size and tart flavor, she'd tirelessly pick them day in and day out until they were all harvested. Late into the evenings, she'd sit watching TV or the news, meticulously cleaning each strawberry. Her hands would be stained bright red, with smudges of berry juice on her clothes, and the occasional squashed berry leaving a tiny stain on the carpet. Perched on the tip of her nose, her cheater

Glasses helped her see as she delicately cleaned each berry while keeping an eye on the show.

Come mid-July, it was time for blueberries, and Mom would disappear daily, spending hours picking the ripe berries. Upon her return, she'd settle into the living room or kitchen, painstakingly cleaning each berry before selling them by the quart or using them to bake pies for family and friends. In later years, my dad joined her in berry picking and even crafted a gadget to assist in cleaning the berries, making the process more efficient.

While Mom also harvested raspberries and blackberries, her true favorites were always strawberries and blueberries. Each winter, she'd transform her bounty into homemade jellies and jams, a labor of love that brought joy to our family's breakfast table throughout the year.

My mom spent time home raising us kids until I was about five. For many years, she worked as a legal secretary. After school, my brother David and I would walk about five blocks downtown from Chisholm High School to the office where she worked. She'd give us gumballs that sat on her desk. We'd go in the back where odd items were stored. There was a fun arcade game, pinball. David and I would fight over who would play it first. It was free to play! Funny, I am 6.5 years older than David, and I was fighting with him over playing pinball. I was so immature.

Mom was brilliant, caring, loving, empathic, and a prayer warrior. She would help strangers, spend time in prayer groups with the ladies in Virginia, go to bible studies, and she would always take time to listen.

I used to playfully tease my siblings about Mom being akin to a gentle lamb, while Dad embodied the strength of a lion. Mom was devout in her reading of the New Testament and made a habit of reading the Bible daily. Her focus was on the teachings found within its pages. In contrast, Dad delved into the prophecy books, with his Bible showing signs of wear primarily around books like Daniel, Ezekiel, and Isaiah.

Dad was renowned among those who knew him for his storytelling prowess. He had a knack for weaving entertaining tales from real-life situations, often turning difficult moments into comedic anecdotes. This gift of storytelling was passed down to my brother David, and I have always admired it.

Before his health setback, Dad worked tirelessly as a foreman at Hibbing Taconite. He seldom spoke about his job, but I remember the demanding shift work he endured, working seven days on each shift rotation: seven days on the day shift (7-3), seven days on the afternoon shift (3-11), and seven days on the night shift (11-7). It was a grueling schedule that left him little time for rest.

Despite his demanding job, Dad made sure to be there for us kids as best he could. He showed his love by providing for us,

cooking meals, and taking us fishing, camping, hunting, and trapping. He had a playful and joking nature, earning him the nickname "kind-hearted Kenny" among family members. While he expressed his love for us in many ways, he struggled to demonstrate it in the way Mom needed and deserved it.

Dad would take us fishing a lot. My mom didn't go fishing until later in life when my parents accepted each other more and took the time to do things together.

I grew close to my dad by trapping in the woods, checking his minnow traps, deer and bird hunting, fishing, and camping. How I wish I paid more attention to the fishing strategies and secret locations. I really enjoyed listening to him talk about the north country and how he shared his knowledge about the land and the lakes.

My mom, on the other hand, was my 'best friend'. She would always listen to me, but sometimes she overstepped caring for me. I think she felt bad and wanted to protect me.

Dad worried too much and would go out driving looking for me if I wasn't home by a specific time. He did this when I was a young adult!

Reflecting on the past, I now understand why my parents acted as they did. They were deeply concerned about me because I was not your typical kid, teenager, or even adult.

One of my favorite stories to share about my parents is how, prior to 1980, they were both struggling and lost souls. Despite attending the Catholic church, they had not yet found a personal relationship with Jesus as their savior. However, everything changed when they received an invitation to attend a Bible group at a friend's home. It was there that they both accepted Jesus into their lives and experienced a profound transformation.

My dad joked that he didn't entirely accept Jesus yet; it wasn't until he was alone in the woods trapping near Fawn Creek North of

Orr, Minnesota, that he went through the ice on the creek. He said, *"I was baptized in the Spirit."* As he chuckled, sharing the story. It's because of my parents' faith and prayers that I grew in my faith as well. My parents' deep-rooted faith and unwavering dedication to prayer and worship have been the cornerstone of my spiritual journey. Their steadfast beliefs and practices have played an instrumental role in shaping my own faith, helping me develop a meaningful connection with Jesus over time.

My Savior

Since my parents accepted Jesus, they attended a different church in the area. They picked a small church called Hibbing Christian Assemblies. Even though I was very young and could barely read, I liked my older siblings' picture bible. I loved looking at the stories about Jesus, especially the one with him and the little children. I don't recall precisely how I accepted Jesus; I just knew I loved him. I was five years old. I loved everything about Sunday school and learned so much. All I wanted to do was learn more about Jesus and the bible and help others know His precious love. I'll never forget when my brother Greg offered to pray with me when I was six years old. He asked, *"Vicky, do you have Jesus in your heart?"* I said, *"I love Jesus; he is in my heart."* Greg offered to help me accept Jesus as my savior, but I already knew him and loved Him dearly.

David

When I was six years old, my mom found out she was pregnant. Total miracle! My mom was 40 for one, plus having a difficult birth with me! I was excited regardless. What was even more remarkable was that two of my aunts were pregnant, too! David grew up having two cousins to hang out with for years. David was my little buddy I played with, babysat, and, as a typical older sister, tormented.

David and I are very close today, and I am very thankful for him. Although younger than me, he has been my unwavering support on numerous occasions. I hold my brother in the highest regard. Together, we have shared an abundance of delightful memories - some of which were amusing and fun, while others were challenging and demanding. I refer to him as my 'lil big brother' because despite being younger than me, he is considerably taller and stronger. I am very proud of him as a veteran of war and supporting his lovely family.

"My childhood was filled with joy and happiness, playing fun activities and creating fond memories even though there were some tough traumatic situations. The horrific events that occurred in my childhood were buried so deep in my mind that it would take years to break free from the bondage that chained my inner child."

Beloved, never avenge yourselves, but leave it to the wrath of God, for it is written, "Vengeance is mine, I will repay, says the Lord." - Romans 12:19

Chapter 7

Of Animals and Such

Golden birthday

When I turned 12, I celebrated my 'golden birthday' by pitching a tent in mid-April, despite the cold weather of Minnesota. It was one of the fondest memories I have of my childhood. I remember inviting 8 to 9 of my friends to spend the night in the tent with me, and despite the chilly conditions, we had a blast. We played games together, including a new board game we had just discovered called Dweebs, Geeks, and Weirdos. We even sang the famous peanut butter jelly song. To keep ourselves warm, I brought along a space heater and a long extension cord, which proved to be just enough to make our overnight adventure both comfortable and fun.

Scary times

One cold November day, seven months after my golden birthday, my dad came home from trapping. It was still early in the morning, and I was getting ready to go to school. My dad came into the house pacing and yelling and in pain. My mom said, *"I will call an ambulance"*, but my dad refused; he was too stubborn. Instead, my sister, Rose, drove my dad to the Hibbing hospital. David and I sat on the couch, watching my dad leave with our big sister. My dad had a massive heart attack and was airlifted from Hibbing to Rochester. He was 49. He shared how he headed North early that morning to check his trap lines North of Orr, MN, when he started to have chest pains. Thankfully, he returned home, but I sure wish he wasn't so stubborn about getting care. Doctors discovered he also had lung issues, probably from working in the mines. The doctors were concerned his lungs couldn't handle bypass surgery, so they completed a balloon angioplasty instead.

This scary event took a toll on our family; we all worried about my dad after that. I started to get anxious and worried about him and prayed he would be ok. Despite my worries, my trust in the Lord remained steadfast, especially after my mom recited a scripture to me that I still remember to this day. Philippians 4

Solace

At the age of 13, my life seemed like a hazy blur. I began to feel an odd sensation and found myself struggling to make friends. Even my closest confidante, Missy, had drifted away towards other social circles. 13 is an arduous age for many adolescents, and it was no exception for me. Frankly, I don't recall much from my seventh through ninth-grade years, but I do know that I felt different from my earlier years. I became quieter, more guarded, and increasingly insecure. My closest friend, whom I once trusted and spent most of my time with, suddenly abandoned our friendship and joined the more popular crowd, her cousin and her new boyfriend. Throughout my life, horses have held a special place in my heart. When I was just 13 years old, my mom noticed that something was off about me - perhaps I was feeling depressed or just going through a tough time. Wanting to ease my troubles, she decided to buy me a horse named Max for $250.

I was overjoyed at the thought of having my very own horse, and I boarded Max in Balkan just North of Chisholm so I could ride him whenever possible. I was determined to take care of him and pay for his boarding with the money I earned from my paper route. The sense of responsibility that came with caring for Max brought me a sense of purpose and connection that I had been missing. He quickly became my trusted companion and a source of comfort during challenging times.

Max was ancient and needed to retire. A horse named Flicka was up for sale. She was a beauty and really good at barrels and gaming. With some careful consideration, I got her, and Max went to a home to retire. Flicka was beautiful, fast, fun, and loved to run!

God's wonderful creation brings me such joy. Whenever the exquisite beauty of nature surrounds me, I feel as though I am in the very presence of the divine. The melodic symphony of birds singing, the gentle rustling of leaves in the breeze, and the breathtaking sight of a sunset all fill me with a sense of peace and a deep spiritual connection to my savior. It's as if nature itself is a manifestation of God's infinite love for us. This connection brings me solace and fills me with a deep sense of gratitude and awe.

As a child, I was drawn to the companionship of animals. From turtles to parakeets, I cherished every pet that I was able to keep. There was even a time when I had a pet chipmunk whom I tried to tame. Animals were my therapy during my formative years, providing me with a sense of comfort and unconditional love that was often missing from human relationships. They never talked back or uttered hurtful words, which made them all the more special to me.

I discovered early on in my life a source of solace and joy in the act of creating art. Whether it be through the medium of drawing, painting, sculpting, writing, or singing, the process of bringing something new into the world is both cathartic and invigorating. Time seems to lose all meaning as I become fully absorbed in the creation process, allowing my mind to wander and explore new ideas. Occasionally, I even pray as I engage with my art, feeling a deep sense of connection and purpose as I bring my innermost thoughts and feelings to life on the page or canvas.

"As I transitioned from my teenage years to early adulthood, life remained full of intrigue. While some memories from my past were marred by trauma, the nostalgia and warmth evoked by my childhood memories are deeply treasured and ever-present in my heart."

Do not be anxious about anything, but in every situation, by prayer and petition, with thanksgiving, present your requests to God. And the peace of God, which transcends all understanding, will guard your hearts and your minds in Christ Jesus. Finally, brothers and sisters, whatever is true, whatever is noble, whatever is right, whatever is pure, whatever is lovely, whatever is admirable—if anything is excellent or praiseworthy—think about such things. Philippians 4:6-8

Chapter 8

Good Times

Turning point

Scott, despite being my ex-boyfriend, remained a consistent and reliable presence in my life even after I ended the relationship. However, we eventually reconciled and resumed our relationship. For a while, everything went smoothly, and I was happy to be with him. In fact, on Thanksgiving Day in the year 2000, Scott proposed to me, expressing his heartfelt gratitude for having me in his life. It was an incredibly touching moment, and I was overjoyed to say "yes." Unfortunately, as time passed, I started to act irritable and irrational again, putting a strain on our relationship. At the time, I wasn't consistently taking the medications I was prescribed (Lithium and Depakote) because I thought I was 'fine.' Due to my belief that I was 'fine,' I ended the relationship with Scott again. To this day, I don't know why I was so irrational. I was hospitalized again in March 2001 due to my hypomania. It wasn't long before I stabilized again, back on the medication and back to my everyday life. But something was missing, and that something was Scott.

After stabilizing on my medication, I received a job offer in the Twin Cities, where I could live with my sister Rose again. Even though Scott and I had broken up, we met one last time. Before I left, he surprised me by returning the engagement ring and asking if I would still like to marry him. Scott is a kind and genuine man, and I couldn't resist his proposal. I said, "Yes, of course!"

Marriage

Life was going great for me. I loved my job as a direct care worker in a group home, and I was engaged to a wonderful man. Being a meticulous planner, I felt excited about coordinating all the details of our upcoming wedding. From the bouquet to the food, I envisioned everything being perfect. We intended to hold the ceremony outside in a pavilion surrounded by water with fountains.

Finally, on August 10th, 2002, we exchanged vows at the Minnesota Discovery Center in the pavilion, with the reception in the building with sliding glass walls to let the beautiful summer air inside. It was a fantastic day, but there was one thing that I'll never forget. During the reception, Scott danced with his mom to the song "I Hope You Dance." I was supposed to dance with my dad too, but I couldn't find him anywhere. After a bit of investigation, I discovered that his feet were hurting from the rental shoes, so he had gone home to change into his comfortable ones. Though I felt a little disappointed, I couldn't help but laugh at the situation.

Bowling

Life was going smoothly for a while. I had tied the knot with a kind and caring man, and I thoroughly enjoyed the jobs I had. Scott was an avid bowler and made it a point to attend bowling nationals every year. I was always there by his side, traveling with him to the tournaments. We preferred to drive, as it allowed us to soak in the picturesque views and make pit stops at various national and state parks along the way. However, as time passed, I started to take these trips for granted. Eventually, I began to harbor some resentment towards Scott. I felt that our love life always revolved around his interests and passions. In hindsight, I realized that this was my fault because I tended to prioritize pleasing others over my own needs and desires.

Volleyball

Volleyball was my passion throughout high school and college. I continued to play in league volleyball starting at age 16. As an adult, I would put together teams for winter and summer leagues.

Scott and I had a regular spot in the church league volleyball every Friday night. It was a tradition my mom had started many years ago, and I always looked forward to it. Apart from that, I also played in the Monday night co-ed league, which was more competitive than the church league. On the other hand, Scott preferred bowling on Mondays. One November night in 2003, while playing in the competitive league, I was receiving a serve when I heard a loud 'pop' from my right knee as I landed. My knee buckled, making it impossible for me to stand up. Thankfully, one of my teammates came to my rescue and carried me off the court.

Made a call, and my mother-in-law arrived to take me to the hospital while Scott was at his bowling league. At the hospital, the emergency room doctor performed a CT scan, revealing that my ACL was torn and my meniscus had buckled, which was why I couldn't put any weight on my leg. The doctor scheduled me for surgery two days later.

Initial injury

When I was nearly 16, I went skiing with my sister Jen and our pastor's family at Giant's Ridge. I tried to ski like the pastor, who was a good skier, but unfortunately, I didn't know how to ski well yet. As a result, I tumbled and tumbled, and my skis flew off. I landed face-down yards down the hill, and my sister saw the whole thing. She thought I was dead or badly hurt because she saw red on my head. However, the red was just my scarf. Although I was okay, my right knee was aching. The ski patrol was contacted, and they arrived with a snowmobile and a sled. They offered to help me lay in the sled, but I was too stubborn and said,

"Nah, I will walk and ride on the back of the snowmobile."

The next day, I went to see my doctor about my swollen knee. After taking an x-ray, he told me there wasn't much he could do except reduce the swelling. He used a syringe with a large needle to drain fluid from my knee, which he had to do twice. The pain was unbearable. In light of the situation, I was given crutches to help keep weight off my swollen knee.

I was disappointed because I did not want to be unable to walk. I spent the day lying in bed, praying and crying, asking the Lord to help me. My junior year had already been challenging, and I felt overwhelmed. I pleaded with the Lord to help me, but since I still couldn't bear the weight of my knee, I continued praying and crying. That night, something changed. I put my whole trust in the Lord, and I was baptized in the Holy Spirit. This moment was life-changing for me. I already loved Jesus, believed in Him, and read the Word, but this experience was remarkable. I will never forget that night.

Horse

In 2004, some friends told me about the Forget-me-not-foundation, which is a facility that uses horses to provide therapy and riding for people with disabilities. Intrigued, I decided to volunteer there and became deeply involved. I spent many evenings caring for the horses, saddling them up, and assisting the riders in any way I could. The facility's caretaker owned a horse named Buddy, a bay horse with a white blaze and three white socks. They were willing to sell him to me, but the problem was that I needed somewhere to keep him. Luckily, the FMNF board agreed to let me keep him there for free if he was trained for the program. I took on the challenge and trained Buddy for the program. Time and patience paid off; Buddy and I volunteered for the program for a few years before I moved him to my friend Nona's in Hibbing, where I boarded him.

Emma

After hearing about a foreign exchange program, I decided to bring some excitement into our lives by inviting an exchange student to stay with us. When I saw the list of kids we could choose from, one girl caught my eye. She had a bright and beautiful smile in her picture, and she was from Australia. Since I've always dreamt of visiting Australia, I thought it would be the perfect opportunity to bring Australia to me. The girl's name was Emma, and she was a fun-loving 15-year-old girl. She arrived in January 2005 and quickly became friends with the girls from our church youth group. Emma even started dating the cute guitar player in the youth group band, named Stephen. Stephen was a great young man, and Emma was intelligent, kind, and very friendly. Emma went back home to Sydney, Australia December 2005, but Stephen continued to occupy her heart. She came back to visit us when she turned 18 and rekindled her relationship with Stephen. Eventually, they started dating again, got married in 2010 in Sydney, and now have children together and live happily ever after in Australia.

"I am grateful for this time in my life; it felt authentic and warming to my soul. Feelings of being on the mountain top."

For the Joy of the Lord is your strength. Nehemiah 8:10

Chapter 9

The Valley

Hospitalization

Taking a turn for the worst, I found myself entangled in a troubling pattern of neglecting my medication regimen. Whether it was due to forgetfulness, inconsistency, or the misguided belief that prayer alone would suffice, I often failed to prioritize my mental health. The details of my hospitalization in Duluth during '06 are hazy, but amidst the fog of uncertainty, one memory shines through—the unwavering support of my niece, Angela. Her presence provided me with a rare sense of comfort, a stark contrast to the usual apprehension that accompanied my interactions with medical professionals and law enforcement.

Unfortunately, encounters with the police became an all-too-frequent occurrence during my manic episodes. Since my initial encounter in '92, a deep-seated fear had taken root within me, triggering a primal instinct to flee. This fear-response only exacerbated the distress of each situation.

While my memory of hospitalization in Brainerd remains fragmented, the unsettling feeling of being adrift in my own mind lingers. Sleep eluded me, and I felt disoriented, a stranger in my own reality. Though the exact year escapes me, the impact of that period remains palpable, serving as a stark reminder of the tumultuous nature of my journey.

Scott

Scott and I had a pretty good relationship. We meshed well together and came from supportive families. However, I had my own battles, probably because of my past traumas, struggles with mental health, and a bit of uncertainty about who I really was. On the other hand, Scott was the epitome of stability - calm, content, and reliable. He enjoyed his job, cherished having his family close by, and found joy in hobbies like bowling and golf. Life seemed pretty smooth sailing for him.

In contrast, I was drawn to variety, excitement, and change. I had a soft spot for animals, especially horses, dogs, and wildlife. I was also creative, dabbling in drawing, painting, writing, and singing. Scott, however, was more pragmatic, focusing on his career as an engineer, loving sports, and relishing travel adventures. Despite our differences, we clicked. But as time passed, I couldn't help but wonder if my struggles with mental health made Scott feel distant at times. Looking back, I realize I needed more understanding and acceptance of myself. I've always been the caregiver, putting others' needs before my own. In hindsight, I believe Scott and I did our best in our marriage. After being married for four years, I met a girl at the park, and we became friends. She had a boyfriend, and the four of us started to hang out together. Scott and I would invite them over for dinner, to sporting events, and to play golf. I was going through a difficult time and didn't realize that I was feeling neglected in my marriage. It wasn't intentional on Scott's part; we didn't have the same mental, physical, or emotional desires.

Foolish

My friend ended things with her boyfriend, and a few weeks later, he invited me to go golfing with him. I mentioned this to Scott, and he was completely fine with it; he's always been trusting and understanding. However, during that outing, I made a mistake. I ended up drinking way too much, something I never do because it's just not me.

I regret it deeply because it led to some regrettable actions with the guy that I'm ashamed to even think about. I even ended up passing out. The guilt and shame consumed me, replaying the scene over and over in my head. Eventually, I couldn't keep it inside any longer, and I tearfully confessed everything to Scott. His response was incredible; he forgave me without hesitation. There was no anger or resentment, just forgiveness. I can only imagine the turmoil he must have felt inside, though.

After that regrettable incident, life seemed to carry on year after year, but deep down, I was far from okay. Despite the outward appearance of having a job, a nice home, a loving husband, and even pets, I felt lost and more broken than ever. While I maintained my faith in the Lord, regularly attending church, praying, and reading the Bible, there was a lingering sense of unease.

Deep within me, there was a wounded little girl who had never truly healed from past abuse and trauma. Unconsciously seeking validation from men and often lashing out due to my own insecurities became patterns in my life. Despite my efforts to find solace in church activities, such as youth leadership, Bible studies, and volunteering to help others, the brokenness within me persisted.

Employment

Despite facing numerous challenges in my life, I never gave up. I always gave my best effort in every situation, even when things seemed impossible. Throughout my career, I primarily worked in the social services field, aiming to make a positive impact on others' lives. However, I also took on a few non-social service jobs from time to time.

Unfortunately, my struggle with manic episodes posed a significant obstacle in my life. Whenever these episodes occurred, I became unstable, making it difficult to maintain employment. This was particularly evident in my early twenties when I frequently lost jobs due to my manic episodes. Despite these challenges, I never lost hope that I would overcome this hurdle and find a path toward stability in both my career and personal life.

I felt a deep sense of self-loathing. I couldn't maintain stability long enough to keep a job or maintain a friendship for an extended period. Have you ever lost a job you really enjoyed? I remember one I had in my twenties as an administrative assistant for a small company. I had many responsibilities and found the work enjoyable, but my mania wreaked havoc. I missed work due to the manic episode and wanted to return, but my family advised me to wait. However, driven by financial concerns and my attachment to the job, I ignored their advice. Because of my erratic behavior and lack of focus, I ended up being terminated. This experience was all too familiar and served as a stark reminder of the challenges posed by managing mania.

"For many years, I carried the burden that I was a bad person. I lived in condemnation, even though Scott forgave me, even though Jesus forgave me. Still, I couldn't see past my adulterous behavior."

Have mercy on me, O God, according to your unfailing love; according to your great compassion, blot out my transgressions. Wash away all my iniquity and cleanse me from my sin. Psalm 51:1-2

Chapter 10

History of My Great Outdoors

Appalachian man

During the early 1980s, my dad had a life-changing encounter while fishing on Lake Vermilion. He met a man with a thick Appalachian accent, which initially posed some difficulty for my dad to comprehend. However, their shared love for the outdoors and a similar sense of humor quickly bonded them into close friends. The Appalachian man from Virginia became a frequent visitor to Minnesota, and he would often return to hunt grouse and whitetail deer with my dad. They spent countless hours together, and my dad shared with him the secrets of the North Woods. Their friendship grew stronger with each passing year, beginning with a simple conversation and a fishing pole.

I, too, enjoyed getting to know my dad's good friend from the South. I learned about the great outdoors from both him and my dad.

Their shared love for hunting strengthened the bond of friendship between my dad and the Appalachian man. In 1999, the man gifted my dad a puppy as a gesture of gratitude. I still remember the day Meg, an English Pointer, arrived at the airport. Her amber eyes were the sweetest I had ever seen, and her coat was as white as snow. She had a large orange spot on her back and some orange on her face. I recall helping my dad train Meg, but it was almost unnecessary as she possessed an innate ability to point and retrieve upland birds.

Bird dogs

In 2003, my dad had the pleasure of meeting Howie, a local hunter, dog trainer, and breeder known for his expertise in breeding and training hunting dogs. After several conversations, they became good friends and decided to breed Meg with Howie's male black and white English Pointer.

Meg gave birth to a litter of eight adorable puppies, half of them black and white and the other half orange and white. I fondly remember spending hours watching them play and develop their own unique personalities. Eventually, I chose a lively black and white male pup, full of energy and curiosity, as my own. Howie assured me that he showed great potential as a bird dog.

We named the little pup Duke, inspired by the popular Dukes of Hazard TV show that my husband Scott enjoyed watching. With Duke joining our family, we now had two hunting dogs, alongside our sweet English Setter, Dixie.

I was determined to train both Duke and Dixie to become the best hunting dogs they could be. I invested countless hours teaching them basic commands, taking them on long walks in the woods, and providing them with the love and care necessary for their development. While the journey wasn't always easy, it was immensely rewarding to witness them grow into the skilled and intelligent hunting companions they are today.

Guide - Grouse Hunting

For many years, every October, my dad would guide a group of hunters from the Appalachian region who came to Minnesota to hunt upland birds. Since Meg couldn't handle too much hunting, my dad asked me to help him guide the group with Dixie and Duke, my two bird dogs. The hunters would stay at Melgeorge's Resort on Elephant Lake, a rustic resort located in the Superior National Forest.

In 2007, a couple of the hunters lost their guide and needed someone to take his place. One of these hunters knew that I had two bird dogs and enjoyed hunting with my dad, so he suggested that I be their guide. I scouted the area and found new locations to hunt. When the hunters arrived in October, my dad and I guided them, and we turned it into a competition to see which group could shoot the most grouse by the end of the day.

We would walk countless trails day in and day out to find grouse and woodcock. Mile after mile, hill after hill, rain, snow, or shine, we were hunting. We would hunt near the Pelican River and trails that always seemed to never end. One trail, which my dad called "wolf hole," held a lot of grouse. He called it wolf hole because one time, while he was hunting with Meg alone, a pack of wolves followed them. I showed the two hunters I guided the Vermilion Falls, a spectacular gorge of water rushing loudly on the Vermilion River just East of Melgeorges Resort. We stopped there when the weather was too hot in the early afternoon to hunt the dogs.

Me hunting with dad Vermillion River overlook

Most days, we would get more birds than my dad's group. Even though he claimed he didn't care, I could tell it bothered his competitive nature. At the end of each day, we always enjoyed a Delicious meal at Melgeorges. We recounted the day's events, each of us telling a good tale. My dad and I decided to have the guys come to Chisholm so we could hunt locally and show them around a little. The day before the guys came to Chisholm, my dad wanted to show me where we would hunt, how he would take his group on the East side of the Iron Ore trails in Chisholm, and how I would take my guys on the West end. We would meet up in the middle.

Well, these trails were around the old mine dumps in Chisholm. Was it simple? Not quite. I had the two guys and Duke, my dog, on this journey. It was a warmer-than-usual day in October. We started our trek on the orange-colored iron ore trails and headed in the direction I thought we were supposed to go. I tried to recall what my dad said. I said to the guys, *"I am not sure we're going the right way. Maybe we should turn around."* The one guy said, *"Nah, we'll be fine."* I kept second-guessing myself, but he wanted to keep going. We walked and walked tirelessly. After hours of walking, one flush from a grouse, I could hear the highway traffic. I finally knew where we were! We were coming up to Highway 169 and the Mesabi bike trail. We walked on the bike trail as we passed by bikers until we got back to Chisholm. We walked for hours on these Iron Ore trails.

The guys were exhausted and sat on a ledge just off the trail while I walked into town. I saw my friend's father-in-law mowing his lawn. I walked up to him and asked him if he could kindly give us all a ride back to my truck parked at the base of the trail a mile or so away. Thank God he did. To this day, I still recount this unforgettable trek. The guys called it 'the death march' and teased me every year after that. I always laugh and tell my family about this favorite memory.

My dogs and the thrill of the hunt

Every year, the arrival of hunting season filled me with excitement and anticipation. I'd eagerly scout new trails, gear up, and set out with our trusty bird dogs by my side. Hunting with these loyal companions was an unparalleled experience. The thrill of the chase, the bond between us, and the satisfaction of a successful hunt made every outing unforgettable.

My bird dogs were true marvels, always ready for the challenge ahead. I trained them diligently to stay within a close range, and when they caught the scent of a grouse, their excitement was palpable. Duke, in particular, was a remarkable sight. His tail would quiver with anticipation when he sensed a bird nearby, and with precision, he'd freeze at a perfect point, his nose leading the way to our quarry.

Once the bird took flight, the real adventure began. Grouse had a knack for darting in unpredictable patterns, making each shot a test of skill and precision. But that was part of the thrill. With careful aim, I'd try to bring down our target, hoping for success. Some might think grouse hunting is as simple as shooting from a dirt road, but the true joy lies in the challenge of hunting with a pointer.

Woodcock hunting held its own allure, especially during peak migration. Unlike grouse, woodcock were less skittish, often waiting patiently before taking off in a unique, helicopter-like flight. Though smaller than grouse, their flight patterns were mesmerizing, adding to the excitement of the hunt. The unmistakable sound of grouse flushing from the cover echoed in my mind, a constant reminder of the thrill of the chase. In the end, hunting with bird dogs was more than just a pastime—it was an adventure I eagerly anticipated each year. The camaraderie, the excitement, and the beauty of nature made every outing a cherished memory, and I wouldn't trade those experiences for anything else.

"I can't put into words how gratifying it was for me to spend time deep in the woods behind my dogs hunting for upland birds. I smile any time I think or talk about the cherished times hunting with my dad and his buddies from the South."

Behold, children are a heritage from the Lord, the fruit of the womb a reward. Like arrows in the hand of a warrior are the children of one's youth. Blessed is the man who fills his quiver with them! - Psalm 127:3-5

Chapter 11

Horses

Bay, Gray, Buckskin

Horse camping became a cherished routine for me, a treasured escape into the wilderness with fellow horse enthusiasts who shared my love for trail riding. There's an unparalleled joy in gathering around the campfire, indulging in s'mores, and swapping stories, all while our faithful horses graze nearby. I boarded my horse with a remarkable lady, Nona, who not only taught me valuable lessons about equines but also imparted wisdom and humor drawn from her deep Christian faith.

When the time came to bring Buddy closer to home from the Forget-Me-Not-Foundation, Nona graciously offered to board him. However, fate had other plans when I crossed paths with a striking young gray horse named Spirit. Despite his youthful awkwardness at just two years old, I couldn't resist his charm. Though Nona proposed selling him to me, I already had Buddy in my care. Yet, the allure of Spirit, especially given his unique Azteca lineage—a blend of quarter horse and Andalusian—proved irresistible. Determined to embark on the journey of training this exceptional horse, I found a loving home for Buddy and welcomed Spirit into my life. Training Spirit was a thrilling journey. Nona's granddaughter, Mollianne, helped me with the training. She was confident and knowledgeable. Every day, I did groundwork with Spirit, eventually getting him used to the saddle and bridle. Next, I had to get on him, which was quite nerve-wracking. At first, everything seemed fine, but then Spirit realized he had all this goofy stuff on him, including me. He gave a little buck here and there, but nothing too crazy. It wasn't until I was riding him around that he gave me some big bucks, throwing me over his head. Thankfully, I never got hurt each time I was thrown off.

As I dedicated myself to training Spirit, I realized the need for a seasoned companion for different equestrian activities like horse shows, parades, and trails. That's when Mischief came into my life. Mischief was a mature horse, seasoned in the ways of the equestrian world. His passion lay in gaming, particularly barrels, where his determination outweighed his speed. Loading him into a trailer was a breeze, and I could confidently ride him solo, away from the comfort of other horses. In every aspect, he was the epitome of perfection.

After months of relentless training, Spirit began to showcase his progress. He mastered the art of neck reining and side passing, evolving into a truly majestic and handsome creature. With his glossy black mane cascading down his neck and his tall, commanding presence, Spirit was a sight to behold. His movements were fluid and graceful, his sleek gray coat adorned with subtle dapples, shimmering under the sunlight.

Now, having two horses that I could ride, I invited others to join me. On one camping trip, my nephew Andrew came along. He rode Mischief while I rode Spirit. Camping with the horse gang was one of my most incredible memories, especially when it involved a HOBO ride.

HOBO, short for horseback orienteering, was a thrilling adventure we eagerly anticipated. Riding in teams of 2 to 5, armed with maps detailing the trails and marked stations, we embarked on a quest to find each checkpoint. Guided by our trusty compasses, we navigated through the wilderness, each station a triumph of skill and teamwork. These events were a highlight for me, filled with camaraderie, exploration, and the joy of discovery. As the day drew to a close, we gathered for a potluck feast, sharing stories and laughter, reliving the excitement of our journey together.

Even though I rode Spirit often to keep him in shape, he couldn't handle the horseback orienteering. He would 'tie up' probably due to electrolyte issues. I would treat him with proper care for this, but he just wasn't suited for endurance-type work. Mischief was a great horse, too, but he developed arthritis.

I loved riding every day and wanted to compete in many types of events, such as gaming, team penning, endurance-type racing, and maybe even mounted shooting. Since neither of my horses fit the bill for this, I decided to sell them. Mischief went to a home for a younger person for lighter riding. Spirit went to a dressage facility. Turns out, he looked just like the owner's original horse. He would do well as a dressage student.

I stumbled upon a gem of a horse named Fancy in North Dakota, a stunning cow-bred beauty primed for success. At just four years old, Fancy boasted a striking buckskin coat and a promising skill set. Eager to bring her home, I enlisted my dad's help for the journey, embarking on a memorable road trip with my Dodge Ram and 16' horse trailer in tow.

As we traversed the miles, I marveled at the countryside unfolding before us, relishing the opportunity to share this adventure with my dad. Upon reaching our destination, I took the reins, guiding us back home through the wintry landscape of early spring in 2010. However, when it came time to maneuver the trailer into its familiar parking spot, my dad faced a challenge amidst the snow-covered terrain.

With a mix of amusement and pride, I stepped in to expertly guide the trailer, showcasing my ability to handle the task with ease. Yet, in hindsight, I couldn't help but chuckle at my fleeting sense of superiority over my dad's momentary struggle. After all, winter's grip was firm, and navigating snowy roads was no easy feat.

Fancy turned out to be the horse I was dreaming of. Fancy would ride out alone, without a care in the world: no hiccups, no issues, just a nice ride, easy to walk, trot, loop, run. Fancy was perfect. There were people in the area starting Mounted Shooting, so I took Fancy there to get her exposed to it. She didn't mind the shooting at all! I helped put the new balloons out during practice and at the county fair. I was so proud of Fancy for being so chill.

When it came to gaming events, Fancy still needed to learn some, but she did her best and moved fast. I brought her to a small horse show in Balkan in May.

"Horses were my therapy, my heart, my way of drawing close to God."

The armies of heaven were following him, riding on white horses and dressed in fine linen, white and clean. -Revelation 19:14

Chapter 12

2010

Content

As the dawn of 2010 unfolded, a profound sense of contentment washed over me, enveloping my life in a warm embrace of fulfillment. Each day seemed to align perfectly with my dreams, especially my cherished ownership of a magnificent horse, a bond I treasured with every ride and tender care I provided. Juggling my two fulfilling jobs felt effortless, granting me the liberty to indulge fully in my passion for horseback riding.

Alongside me, my loyal companion Duke, my faithful canine friend, remained a steadfast presence, infusing each moment with boundless joy and companionship. Blessed with a close-knit circle of friends who shared my passion for equestrian pursuits, we reveled in the freedom of endless rides through sprawling countryside vistas. In the sanctuary of our home, presided over by my unwavering husband, tranquility reigned supreme, offering solace and security in every corner. It was a time of abundance, a chapter in my life overflowing with gratitude for each precious moment bestowed upon me.

Memorial Day Ride

In the early summer of 2010, I made a bold decision to host a HOBO (horseback orienteering) ride over Memorial Day weekend when everyone would be camping with their horses. On the day of the HOBO setup, I set out with my horse-loving friend Mollianne and her 4-wheeler, as well as two other enthusiastic horse-loving girls who were there to assist us.

As we made our way along the trails, we came across a trail that was incredibly steep uphill. Sensing the danger that lay ahead, I asked the girls to wait and let me go up the hill alone first. With my trusty 4-wheeler, I began the ascent.

But then, disaster struck. As I reached the middle of the hill, my tire caught on a large rock, causing the 4-wheeler to shimmy to the right at a substantial angle. Instinctively, I jumped off and rolled away from the 4-wheeler. Everything happened so quickly that I barely had time to think, let alone react.

As I lay there on the ground, I prayed out loud, *"Jesus, help!"* And then, with a loud crash, the 4-wheeler flipped and rolled, coming to a stop right next to me. The other girls watched in amazement as they stated that the 4-wheeler was going to land on me, but it tipped and landed next to me instead. It was a close call, but by some miracle, we had all escaped unscathed.

We arranged a fun-filled HOBO ride with a patriotic theme. The participants' feedback was mixed, as some found it to be too easy, while others relished the challenge. Despite this, we thoroughly enjoyed putting it all together and making it a success.

However, during the camping weekend, I had a restless night and ended up chatting all night with a couple of the girls. It was a casual conversation and didn't seem like a significant event at the time. Nonetheless, the beautiful night sky, the sound of the Minnesota wildlife, and the warmth of the campfire made the experience unforgettable.

June

On Tuesday, June 8th, the routine hum of my workday at the nursing home was suddenly shattered by a missed call notification from my mom at 9:27 am. Sensing urgency, I resolved to return her call promptly during my morning break at 9:30 am, only to be met with silence on the other end. Concern gnawed at my insides as the clock ticked past noon, and my brother David's unexpected call sent a chill down my spine. His words cut through the air like a sharp knife – Dad had returned home to find Mom unresponsive.

Without a second thought, I abandoned my tasks and dashed out the door, leaving a trail of unanswered questions in my wake. Ignoring the speed limits, I raced from Hibbing to Chisholm, the distance between them reduced to a blur in my frantic haste. Amidst the chaos of my racing thoughts, I reached out to Scott for support, but his commitment to work left me grappling with the weight of uncertainty alone. When I arrived at my parents' home, an ambulance was parked outside. As I walked inside, I was greeted by a paramedic who said, *"I'm sorry, Vicky."*

I glanced to my right and saw my dad, still clad in his tan spring coat and black shoes, sitting on the couch, tears streaming down his face uncontrollably. The paramedic by his side was diligently assessing his vitals, mindful of his own health issues.

My dad's trembling voice broke the heavy silence as he uttered those haunting words, *"She's gone."* His tears bore witness to the depth of his anguish. Numbness gripped me as I made my way into my parent's bedroom, where a scene of heart-wrenching finality awaited me.

There, on the floor beside the bed, lay my dear mom, her life extinguished in the blink of an eye. The phone lay abandoned by her side. With a heavy heart, I knelt beside her, my soul echoing with grief, and pressed a gentle kiss upon her forehead.

Through tear-streaked eyes, I whispered those three words that now carried an unbearable weight, *"I love you, Mom."* At that moment, as I bid farewell to the woman who had been my guiding light, I was overwhelmed by the stark reality of her absence. Sixty-six years of life, love, and laughter now reduced to a memory etched in the depths of my soul.

The coroner's grim verdict confirmed our worst fears – Mom had suffered a massive heart attack. The pieces of the puzzle started to fall into place as we pieced together the events leading up to her untimely passing. Mom's call to my sister Jen earlier that morning, expressing her discomfort, followed by attempts to reach out to me while I was at work, now haunted us with questions. Could those missed calls have been the desperate cries for help as the heart attack took hold?

As evening descended, our family home became a sanctuary for a flood of emotions. Gathered together were not just relatives but a tapestry of cherished souls whose lives had been touched by Anita Hope (Chase) Rosc. Amidst tears and laughter, we shared stories of her boundless love and unwavering faith. Anita's legacy was one of compassion and empathy, always willing to lend an ear and offer solace to those in need. Her fervent prayers were a testament to her deep-rooted faith, while her endearing habit of fumbling jokes and laughing at herself endeared her to all. Whether she was out picking berries with Dad or engrossed in her beloved Bible, Anita's presence radiated warmth and love. But above all, she was my confidante, my mentor, and my rock – my best friend and beloved mom.

I'm uncertain why, but I began planning Mom's funeral. I took charge; not once did I cry or mourn her death.

As the child living closest to my parents, it made sense for me to take on this responsibility. However, I also recognize that I shared a similar trait with my mom - the coordinator. Despite the emotional weight of the situation, I felt a sense of duty and

125

determination to organize a beautiful farewell for our beloved mom, Anita.

I remember that after my mom passed away, I met with my siblings and the funeral home to make arrangements for her funeral. We also practiced a song that we planned to sing at her funeral. During this time, I was very forthright with everyone around me. It didn't matter the discussion; I was blunt. At the time, I didn't notice how I was towards others; I was just taking charge of the matter.

Everyone was experiencing many emotions, from extreme tears to belly laughter, sharing stories about Mom. My dad was broken and could barely function. My brother David held him in bed, my siblings crying and crying. I had no emotion; I just focused on making sure all was well and planned just right. I'm sure I was in shock. Not once did I cry before, during, or after Mom's funeral.

My parent's pastor officiated her funeral. Greg played piano while all five of us siblings sang a beautiful song. I sang with a big smile on my face as if I was full of joy. I don't know if that was joy or simple shock.

After the funeral, the family was invited to my house for a post-funeral reception. I was engrossed in taking care of matters of my mom's past bills and such instead of spending time with family. It's like a switch went off in my brain, and I couldn't help but take charge and get it all done.

Give me a break

While I grappled with the challenges of losing my mom and organizing her funeral, a seemingly innocuous comment about my cooking skills hit me hard, adding to my emotional burden. Feeling overwhelmed, I reached out to my dad's old friend, who kindly offered me refuge at his home with his wife. Despite my financial worries, I made the decision to sell my 4-wheeler to finance my trip to the Appalachian man's residence.

Upon arrival, I was captivated by the serene beauty of the Virginia countryside. The Appalachian man and his wife greeted me warmly, sharing cherished memories of my dad and their hunting escapades. They introduced me to their sister-in-law Tara and her husband John, who lived nearby and were avid horse enthusiasts. Spending time with them was a balm to my soul, offering solace and companionship amid my grief.

One particular moment with John remains etched in my memory. He spotted a vibrant June bug and, with nimble fingers, affixed a string to one of its legs. As he set it free, the June bug soared into the air, its iridescent wings glimmering in the sunlight. I watched in wonder as it darted gracefully, resembling a miniature helicopter in flight. Amidst this enchanting scene, I found myself laughing joyously, momentarily lifted from the weight of my sorrow, as I savored the simple beauty of the moment over a glass of Southern sweet tea. One day, the Appalachian man and his wife took me on a hike to the White Rocks and Sand Cave, which offered stunning views and unique sand. Despite the challenging trek, I found it to be a worthwhile and memorable experience.

As we ventured through the White Rocks, I was mesmerized by the stunning vistas that unfolded before my eyes. The gleaming quartz and rugged limestone cliffs stood out against the vivid blue sky, creating a mesmerizing contrast that felt like a masterpiece crafted by God himself.

The Sand Cave was another marvel that left me in awe. Formed from centuries of erosion, its sandy interior sparkled in the sunlight like a hidden treasure waiting to be discovered. The tranquil waterfall cascading over the cave provided a refreshing mist, soothing our weary souls after the long hike.

Surrounded by a lush blanket of Rhododendron and Hemlock pines, the area felt like a sanctuary, teeming with vibrant wildlife. It was a truly magical experience, where nature's beauty unfolded at every turn, leaving an indelible mark on my heart and mind.

Home, but is it home?

Upon returning from my trip to the Appalachian region, I felt revitalized and ready to resume my daily routine at work and home. Despite the absence of my mom, everything appeared normal to me, even though the shock of her passing still heavily weighed on my mind. I overly cared for everyone but myself. I strived to be the best at everything I did. I people pleased, I yearned to be liked. I was in shock from my mom's death. I wanted to take care of my family, but I didn't know if anyone was taking care of me, especially myself. I did everything I usually did, like show my artwork at the fair, bring my horse to the fair, clean the house, work my job, and try to be a good wife. It all caught up to me. I was hospitalized in the psychiatric unit on July 25th for three days and again on July 31st for three days. I believe church friends were concerned by my behavior and called the police both times.

One afternoon in late July, I got into an argument with Scott. To this day, I don't remember everything we discussed; the only thing I do remember is my asking for a divorce. If I recall correctly, Scott said to me that I was manic. I never saw myself that way, nor did I ever recognize it, regardless of the manic episode I was in.

All I remember is the argument ending with, *"Fine, we will get a divorce."*

I can only imagine some things I said; they were probably hurtful and off. Oh, how I wish I could control my state of mind and the words that spewed from my mouth due to my crazy mania.

The argument Scott and I had may have been the one' big one' we truly ever had. We never argued while we dated or while we were married for eight years. The only struggle was when I was manic. Scott and I dated off and on for eight years, with me ending it three times during those eight years. I struggled through those eight years, but I always loved him, and I believe he always loved me. We had a decent marriage, 'status quo.' It all appeared good. He is a nice guy who has everything together; I, on the other hand, am a quirky, moody person. He and I were different.

Needless to say, that's not a bad thing, but we had our issues that we never faced. I'm sure Scott loved me the best he could. For many years, I blamed myself for everything. I was 'crazy' dealing with bipolar periodically. He had to try to 'deal' with me when I was manic. Maybe deep down, I felt somewhat abandoned or rejected. I wasn't myself when I was manic, and I was a broken person while Scott and I were together.

Scott and I went to the courthouse, filled out the paperwork together, paid the fee, filed for divorce, and in a matter of days, we were divorced—August 11th, 2010, ironically a day after our anniversary.

I didn't ask for much in the divorce. Scott suggested that I get the truck since I owned a horse and trailer. Although Scott kindly offered to pay alimony, I refused it because I didn't want to be dependent on him. My only requests were 10% of the value of our house and a few specific items, like the old recliner and a stereo system.

When my marriage ended, I decided to change my name. Besides, it didn't cost extra to do so in divorce. As a child, I always admired the name Victoria. But when I asked my mom why she named me Vicky instead of Victoria, she replied, *"Victoria is very proper and British. You're not proper, you're just Vicky."*

This made me feel sad and disappointed. The name Victoria had a special meaning to me, and I associated being called Vicky with mental illness and teasing, so I decided to change it.

My married name was Vicky Lee Fawkes, and I changed it to Victoria Rosc, dropping my middle name in the process. My relative, who often teased me, would call me, *"Vicky Lee Chinese Laundry Lady,"* so I decided to drop the middle name altogether.

After my divorce, I rented a townhome in Hibbing, but I still felt restless and uneasy. I had a job at a nursing home, but they were laying off people at the end of August, and a newer colleague would lose her job. She expressed that she couldn't afford to be cut due to taking care of her family. I volunteered to quit so that she could keep her job.

"Mom, she was amazing at loving people right where they were at. She genuinely loved with all she had, even through her own brokenness. I am so thankful she was my mom."

She dresses her arms with strength and makes her arms strong. She opens her hand to the poor and reaches out to the needy... A woman who fears the Lord is to be praised. - Psalm 31:17, 20, 30

My mom, Anita, and I fishing on Pelican Lake

Chapter 13

New Beginnings

Journey South

After building a friendship with Tara during my visit to Virginia in July, we continued to stay in touch. During our conversations, I expressed my desire for change. I was tired of living on the Iron Range and felt like I didn't belong there anymore. Tara kindly offered me and my horse, Fancy, a place to live so I could start over.

August 31st was my last day working at the nursing home. I broke my lease with the landlord of the townhome, and Scott allowed me to stay on his couch for my final night on the Iron Range. I had all my belongings in my truck and horse trailer, parked outside, ready to go.

I woke up early before sunrise, drove to where I boarded my horse, Fancy, and loaded her up. I had hay and water packed away so that Fancy would have what she needed as we headed South for a 16-hour drive, covering over 1000 miles.

I embarked on the long and arduous journey, driving non-stop, arriving at Eau Claire, Wisconsin. Exhausted and in need of a break, I tended to my beloved horse, Fancy, providing her with ample hay to eat and a refreshing drink of water. While she rested, I fueled up my trusty truck and grabbed a quick bite to eat. Our journey resumed, and we made another stop in Illinois at a truck stop where we decided to spend the night. I slept in the truck, constantly waking up to check on Fancy, ensuring she was comfortable and safe. The next day, I felt an overpowering sense of excitement, knowing that we would finally be arriving in Virginia later that day.

Nestled in the heart of the Tri-state region where the states of Virginia, Tennessee, and Kentucky converge lies Tara's humble abode. Located in the southwestern tip of Virginia, her home is surrounded by stunning natural beauty and rich cultural heritage. From the hollers in the verdant forests to the vibrant local communities, Tara's home lies in a true gem of the region. Her home exudes a sense of serenity and natural beauty. The gentle sound of a meandering creek flows through the property, adding to the peaceful ambiance. The surrounding landscape is a picturesque blend of rolling hills and majestic old mountains, creating a breathtaking backdrop for my idyllic new home.

Tara gently led Fancy into the spacious round pen, where she was introduced to her new equine companions. The pen provided a safe and enclosed environment for Fancy to interact and bond, allowing Fancy to become more familiar with Tara's two horses.

I stepped inside Tara's house, and my eyes were immediately drawn to the stunning decor that adorned every corner of her home.

The vibrant colors of the throw pillows and the delicate intricacy of the wall art were captivating, just as they were when I last visited in July.

As I ascended the stairs to the upper floor of the house, I couldn't help but feel a sense of excitement. It was going to be my own personal space. The loft-like bedroom was cozy yet spacious, and the tiny bathroom was just enough to meet my needs. The entire house was filled with horse paintings, horse decor, and everything horse-related, which I found charming. But the big red barn was the real gem of the property. It had a rich history and was previously used to hang dry tobacco. The boards of the barn were built with a gap between them, adding to its rustic charm.

The following day, I went to see how Fancy was. As I gazed into the distance, I caught sight of an old mountain hillside. The lush greenery of the trees was slowly giving way to the warm hues of autumn, with shades of orange and yellow painting the landscape. The roads snaked and wound their way through the area, meandering between the ranches and homes that dotted the surroundings. The peaceful and serene setting was a sight to behold, and I couldn't help but feel a sense of calm and tranquility wash over me.

While I was watching Fancy, Tara came outside and greeted me and Fancy with a warm smile and wished us a good morning. We started chatting about our shared love for horses. Tara told me about her two beloved horses - Jack, a Chestnut colored Tennessee Walker with a small star on his face, who was a smooth rider, and Tilly, a robust sorrel quarter horse with a gentle spirit. Jack's coat shimmered like a brand-new penny. We decided to go to the barn to feed the horses together before heading in for breakfast.

Over breakfast, I asked Tara and her husband if they knew of any job openings in the area. I shared that I had worked in a nursing home before and wanted a job ASAP. Tara mentioned a nursing home in Middlesboro, Kentucky, which was about 20 miles away.

Riding in the Hollers and Kentucky job

As the morning sun shone on the rolling hills, I spent the morning with Tara and our horses. After bidding farewell to them, I drove towards Middlesboro. I passed through the town and down a long street, enjoying the scenery as I went. Eventually, I reached the nursing home, which was nestled among large oak trees.

As I stepped inside, I was struck by the elegant decor and soothing atmosphere of the place. A large plaque on the wall caught my attention, proudly announcing that the nursing home had been voted the best in the area. The sounds of a baby grand piano drifted towards me from the right, and I couldn't resist peeking over to see it. A kind lady in the reception area greeted me with a charming Appalachian accent and asked how she could help me. She handed me an application, which I quickly filled out. A few moments later, I was greeted by the hiring manager, who offered me a job on the spot. I was overjoyed and couldn't believe it. The hiring manage asked me to start working the following Monday. I left the nursing home with a spring in my step, already eager to begin my new job.

The following day, Tara suggested that we take our horses out for a ride. She led Tilly into the stall in the barn while we prepared Jack and Fancy for the ride. I was thrilled as I got on Fancy, feeling the saddle beneath me and the bridle in my hand. Tara mounted Jack, and we set off into the breathtaking scenery. The trail took us to the quarry pond, several miles away from the house. As we got closer, the quarry's turquoise and teal hues came into view, making it look like a vast ocean of shimmering water. We couldn't help but giggle as we chatted about life and our love for horses while enjoying the beautiful surroundings.

Upon our return, we untacked the horses, and after cooling them down, we let them out to pasture with the creek. We then headed to the house to quench our thirst with a tall glass of sweet Southern tea. We sat under the tulip trees' shade to relax, taking in the peacefulness of our surroundings. I felt so relaxed here, as if time had slowed down. Unlike in Minnesota, there was no rushing or hurrying about. We sat there, basking in the late summer breeze, watching the sun slowly set to the West. It was as if time and the past didn't exist.

The start of the week brought with it new beginnings for me as I began my employment at the Middlesboro nursing home. The location was nothing short of picturesque, and it was evident that the elderly residents found solace in calling it their home. From the moment I arrived, I was struck by the warm and welcoming atmosphere that permeated the place. The staff and residents alike were all incredibly kind and considerate, and there was an air of gentleness that was difficult to come by in this day and age. It was refreshing to be in a place where time seemed to slow down, and people took the time to appreciate the simple things in life.

I worked four days a week at a nursing home, where I would clean rooms and assist with activities. On my days off, I would often go horseback riding on my beautiful mare, Fancy, or explore the surrounding area to get to know it better. To reach the town of Middlesboro from my home in Virginia,

Had to traverse the awe-inspiring Cumberland Gap tunnel. Descending into the depths of this nearly one-mile-long, four-lane passage, I felt a surge of exhilaration and anticipation. Each journey through this remarkable tunnel was an adventure in itself, leaving a lasting impression on me.

Middlesboro served as my go-to destination for supplies, prompting frequent drives for groceries and essentials. Yet, I welcomed these trips eagerly, relishing the chance to traverse the tunnel once more. Alternatively, if I opted for Harrogate, Tennessee, the convenience stores there offered only limited options.

Cumberland Gap

Every day, while driving on Highway 58 as it intersects with Highway 25E, I saw a glimpse of the majestic Cumberland Gap. Intrigued by its beauty, I decided to make a stop at the quaint little town of Cumberland Gap. As I turned onto Cowlyn Avenue and parked in front of the post office, I couldn't contain my excitement to explore the charming streets of this hidden gem. The picturesque scenery and peaceful atmosphere of the town instantly made me feel at home.

Embarking on my adventure around Cumberland Gap, I eagerly ventured into each building, eager to soak in the essence of the area. Amidst my exploration, I stumbled upon a rejuvenating creek nestled on the north edge of town, offering a serene oasis, and a meticulously restored historic mill, now transformed into a quaint bed and breakfast.

Engaging with the locals, I was struck by their genuine warmth and hospitality. Each conversation revealed a deep reverence for the town's storied past, particularly its role during the Civil War. Immersed in their tales, I felt a profound connection to this enchanting locale, a place where history and community intertwined seamlessly.

Cumberland Gap is undeniably one of the most historical places in the United States and is adjacent to Cumberland Gap

National Park. The natural beauty of the area is awe-inspiring, and it's no wonder that it has become such a popular tourist destination.

As I continued my walk, I stopped at a quaint bike shop where I had a delightful conversation with the owner, an elderly gentleman who knew the area like the back of his hand. I was so enamored with this town that I even contemplated living here. However, I didn't want to continue to impose on Tara and her husband, so I asked the kind bike store owner if he knew of a place to rent. To my surprise, he had an apartment upstairs that was available for rent. I was overjoyed and made plans to discuss the details further with him the following day.

During our conversation, I mentioned that I was an artist, and he suggested that I visit a big brick house down the street that was a frame shop and sold artwork. I was intrigued and decided to take a look. As I walked down the street, I couldn't help but admire the beautiful two-story brick house with its stunning white columns around the wrap-around porch. As I walked in, the bell on the door chimed, announcing my arrival. The walls of the shop were adorned with an array of large and small artwork, and a tall gentleman with glasses greeted me with a smile. I gleefully said, *"What a nice place you have here, and I am an artist!"*

He responded with, *"Looks like you're in the right place,"* as he smiled.

I introduced myself as Victoria, but I used to go by Vicky. The gentleman, whose name was Steve, shared that he was the owner of the shop and enjoyed framing artwork and striking up conversations with customers.

As we chatted, I shared that I was originally from Minnesota but had recently moved to Virginia for a fresh start. I had just started a new job in Middlesboro, and I was excited to talk about it. Steve was a great listener and asked thoughtful questions.

Before we parted ways, I mentioned that I would love to show him some of my artwork someday. Steve seemed genuinely interested and agreed to take a look. As I left the shop, I couldn't help but feel grateful for the friendly and welcoming encounter I had just experienced.

As the day came to an end, I returned to my humble home in Virginia. My mind was buzzing with excitement as I looked forward to sharing my experience at the Gap with Tara. The setting sun cast a warm, golden glow across the sky as I walked through the door, eager to recount my adventure. We sat down to enjoy a plate of steaming hot spaghetti and juicy meatballs, savoring each bite of the delicious meal while chatting animatedly about our day. The cozy atmosphere of my home, combined with Tara's warm company, made it a perfect evening spent together.

The next morning, I shared my plan to move to Cumberland Gap with Tara and her husband. They liked the idea and even offered to take care of Fancy so that I could visit and go for rides whenever I wanted. I went back to Cumberland Gap to talk with the owner of a bike store about renting an apartment. He showed me a one-bedroom, one-bathroom apartment with an open kitchen and living room area and offered me a good deal for rent. It was the perfect size for just me.

Since the apartment was unfurnished, I went to a local store to get the necessary furniture. It was heartwarming to see how people came out of the woodwork to help me move the furniture. After getting settled in, I paid a visit to Steve at the frame shop. Steve was in the middle of a flurry of activity, helping customers, taking orders, and answering phone calls. Despite the hustle and bustle, he took the time to chat with me about his work and how busy he gets. As we talked, we realized that I could help him out by working there part-time. We went over the details and made a plan for me to start soon.

During my time at the frame shop, I was faced with a number of challenges that made my work both interesting and rewarding. Steve, was incredibly patient as I worked on preparing each piece for him. While I focused on the basics, Steve took on the more difficult tasks, allowing me to learn and grow within my role. All in all, it was an enlightening experience that taught me a great deal about the art of framing.

Fancy at her finest

I had the pleasure of working part-time at both the nursing home and the Frame Shop, but my heart was always with my horse, Fancy. Every chance I got, I would ride her through the countryside. One day, while I was out on a ride, Tara's husband mentioned that a neighbor's cow was on the loose. I saw it as an opportunity to put Fancy's cow-herding skills to the test.

As we rode down the winding road, I spotted the black Angus cow grazing along the roadside. I positioned Fancy in front of the cow's right shoulder and gently nudged it in the direction of home. The cow barely moved, but I urged Fancy on, and after a few minutes, the cow began to trot away from us.

Fancy and I continued to steer the cow, making sure to keep it moving in the right direction. Suddenly, the cow lost its patience and head-butted Fancy in the left shoulder. To my surprise, Fancy didn't even flinch and continued to push the cow towards the fence.

We eventually made it to the fence line, and the cow hopped over the low fence. It felt like we had accomplished something great, and I was grateful for the opportunity to put Fancy's skills to the test.

New Friends

I went to find a church that resonated with me. My initial attempt at a Baptist church left me feeling out of place, dressed casually amidst a sea of Sunday best attire. It simply didn't click.

However, one day, a sign for a non-denominational church caught my eye, sparking my curiosity. Stepping inside, I was enveloped by a sense of belonging. The congregation greeted me with open arms, and the ambiance exuded warmth and acceptance.

The sermon touched my soul, speaking directly to my heart. During the service, I had the pleasure of meeting a compassionate elderly missionary who shared his inspiring story of adopting two teenagers from Brazil. Instantly, we connected, spending time getting to know each other after the service. Eager to continue our newfound friendship, I extended an invitation for lunch, and we headed to the Cracker Barrel together with his two adopted children.

During my time with the missionary and family, we established a great connection and continued to nurture it even after church services. Our bond grew stronger as we spent time together during the week, sharing stories, ideas, and experiences.

Ferrier

The time came for a much-needed trim for Fancy and Tara's horses. Tara had previously mentioned her farrier in our conversations and had described him as a kind and friendly person. She would often joke about him being single, winking suggestively. At the time, I was unsure about my feelings about dating, but I decided to keep an open mind As we waited for the farrier, I couldn't help but feel a sense of anticipation. Finally, Rick arrived in his Ford pickup, and I couldn't help but notice his tall stature and his striking black hair with a thin goatee. He had an air of confidence and experience about him as he approached the horses to begin their trim. He was pleasant to talk to, but I was hesitant about anything more than another acquaintance.

A week later, Tara invited him over for some tea and a visit. We all chatted about life and the beautiful day. Rick offered to take me hunting after I mentioned I hunted back in Minnesota. I took him up on the offer, and we went deer hunting not too far away. We sat quietly next to a broad oak tree and sat in anticipation. As the sun was setting and dusk set in, we could hear soft crunches to our left. Sure enough, a doe. It was too dark, and I didn't have a clear shot, so we just watched her walk over the hill. *"Next time,"* he said. Afterward, we got a bite to eat and visited.

We struck up a friendship and spent time together at Tara's and with the horses. He even rode a horse with us a couple of times to the quarry and other trails.

Tara, Rick, and I embarked on an unforgettable trail ride that took us on a scenic route. We rode along a winding road that meandered past charming cottages and small farms. Along the way, we were greeted by towering sycamore and oak trees that cascaded the hillsides, providing us with awe-inspiring views. The sound of a nearby creek added to the peaceful ambiance of the ride. After some time, we reached a trailhead and began riding our horses up a steep incline, with the promise of even more breathtaking sights. It was

145

then that I noticed something concerning - my horse, Fancy, was struggling on the rocks due to not having horseshoes on. Taking this into account, we decided to turn back and head home. Despite the early end of our ride, the memories we made on the trail will stay with me forever.

The region where I resided, encompassing three different states, was a place of unparalleled beauty. Each day, I woke up to a job that filled my heart with joy - working at a lavish nursing home, as well as for Steve at his Frame Shop. In my leisure time, I took pleasure in exploring the awe-inspiring trails of Cumberland Gap National Park, which provided me with a sense of tranquility and serenity. One of the most delightful things I did was to ride Fancy, my sweet-tempered buckskin, while spending time with Tara and Rick, the skilled Ferrier. And on Sundays, I continued to enjoy visiting the kind-hearted missionary and his family.

Christmas 2010

During the festive season of Christmas, I was invited to spend time with the missionary and his family. I offered to cook tacos, and they gladly accepted. While preparing the dish, I noticed that they didn't have a packet of taco seasoning, so I gathered all the seasonings I could think of making it from scratch. The taste was exquisite, with just the right balance of flavors, albeit a tad less salty.

The adopted children from Brazil excitedly cried out, *"Victoria, look out the window; it's snowing!"* I turned my head towards the window and was greeted with the mesmerizing sight of large, fluffy snowflakes gracefully falling from the sky.

They covered everything in a pristine white blanket, transforming the outside world into a winter wonderland. However, amidst this breathtaking beauty, a wave of sadness and melancholy suddenly swept over me, realizing how deeply I missed my dear mom. It was as if a veil had been lifted, and the weight of her absence hit me like a ton of bricks. The stark reality of her being gone hadn't truly sunk in until that moment, as I watched the snow falling outside.

I turned to the missionary, seeking solace, and asked if it was alright to lie down for a moment. As I lay there, gazing at the gentle dance of snowflakes, a flood of emotions overwhelmed me. Tears streamed down my cheeks as I longed for home, missing my family, my dad, and even Scott. It was a stark realization – all this time, I had been living in a state of shock, as if Mom's passing had never truly occurred.

"What did I do?" I thought. I got divorced, and my mom was gone. I left a good home and life behind. Depression crept into my soul, and a weight more significant than a pillar overcame me. I called my dad, saying through my tears, *"Dad, I am so sad; I miss Mom; I just want to come home."*

He replied, *"Come home, Vicky, come home."*

I said, *"I can't. There's no way I can drive back alone. Can I get you a flight to come here?"* He said he would do that.

I called the nursing home and quit my job on the spot; I said, *"My mom died, and I can't work."* It wasn't a lie, just timing. My reality was a form of shock mixed with mania after Mom passed. I also called Steve, informing him I was going to move back to Minnesota. He said he understood.

My state of depression weighed heavily on me, to the point where I made decisions that seemed unthinkable under normal circumstances. I instructed the landlord of my apartment to give away the furniture, feeling an overwhelming sense of detachment from material possessions. Even giving away Fancy, my beloved horse, to the Ferrier Rick, seemed like the only option in my clouded state of mind, despite knowing her considerable value.

When my dad's flight touched down at Knoxville airport, I eagerly awaited his arrival, yearning for his comforting presence. His Appalachian friend graciously offered him a place to stay, and as we pulled up to the house, I witnessed a glimmer of joy in my dad's eyes at the sight of his friend's cozy abode. Over the next few days, they shared precious moments catching up and reminiscing before we started on our journey back home to Northern Minnesota. With my essential belongings, saddle, and tack packed into my horse trailer, we set out on the road, ready to face whatever lay ahead.

As we pulled into Minnesota on December 31st, 2010, the wintry landscape greeted me with its pristine white expanse and biting cold. It was a stark contrast to the journey we had just completed, a reminder of the familiarity that awaited me in my childhood home. Amidst the flurry of unpacking, I positioned my horse trailer beside the garage, its once vibrant maroon exterior now dulled by the wear and tear of the road. Aware of the harsh Minnesota winter, I hurriedly brought my saddle and tack indoors, shielding them from the frigid air.

Climbing the stairs, I found solace in the familiarity of my childhood room. The well-worn mattress and the comforting embrace of the green floral blanket welcomed me back, offering a sense of comfort in the midst of uncertainty.

Reflecting on the year that had passed, I couldn't shake the feeling of being caught in the strangest kind of whirlwind. Despite functioning relatively normally and holding down a job, I couldn't ignore the underlying sense of disquiet that lingered within me. Looking back, I realized that I had been navigating through a state of shock for the past six months, grappling with emotions that I couldn't quite comprehend.

This experience may have been due to shock, but as someone reported to me, I showed signs of mania prior to my mom's passing. I am uncertain if I was starting to become manic before she passed or not. I do know, though, that this was a form of mania. I was able to work and act normal, but yet I wasn't quite right. By far, this was the strangest manic episode I ever experienced.

"For many years, the events of 2010, losing my mom and the divorce left my heart broken in many pieces regardless of what I showed on the outside."

The Lord is close to the brokenhearted and saves those who are crushed in spirit. - Psalm 34:18

Chapter 14

2011

Glimmers of hope while Mourning

My life had undergone a significant change, and I found myself spending most of my days idly lounging around. A feeling of hopelessness and apathy engulfed me, and it seemed as though nothing mattered anymore. In an attempt to rid myself of this feeling, I decided to sell everything related to my passion for horses. First, I auctioned off my horse trailer, then all my tack, and finally, my cherished saddle. I had spent a considerable amount of money on it, selling off two valuable saddles to afford it. It had been a perfect fit for both me and my horse, Fancy. However, at that moment, it's worth held little significance to me. I made a hasty decision and sold everything for much less than their actual value.

My dad did the best he could to encourage me, 'dad style,' even though he, too, was struggling emotionally and grieving mom's death. He would say to me as I lay mournfully on the couch, *"Go put makeup on; you'll feel better." "Get a job, that'll help."* We both struggled with our grief; we just handled it differently. I did listen to my dad, and I got hired in February to work in a group home doing direct care. My sister-in-law, Kim, extended an invitation to visit her family in the Twin Cities area. I had been looking forward to the trip because it was a chance to finally meet the guy, Kangas, I had been talking to over the phone for a couple of months. We had great conversations, and I was eager to see if we would hit it off in person. Daily, I struggled with depression, but I always looked forward to my phone conversations with Kangas. He and I both had been through some tough times and understood each other.

We arranged to meet at a cozy restaurant not far from Kim's parents' house. When I arrived, I saw him waiting for me with a friendly smile on his face. He was kind and funny, and I felt immediately at ease in his presence.

As we enjoyed our meal together, he caught me off guard by unveiling a sketchbook. To my astonishment, he had sketched a portrait of me donning my beloved cowboy hat, a detail he had spotted in one of my online photos. The portrait was incredibly lifelike, capturing every subtle contour of my face with remarkable precision. I was struck by his artistic prowess, a talent I admired and wished I possessed, as my artistic endeavors typically gravitated toward animals and landscapes.

After our meal, Kim arrived to pick me up, and I eagerly shared with her the stunning portrait he had gifted me. Together, we admired his skill and creativity, both agreeing that it was one of the most delightful surprises I had ever received My dear brother David has always been there for me. In May, he suggested that I should get a furry companion of my own. He spoke about how dogs bring joy, love, and companionship, and it might make me feel better. Unfortunately, I gave up my beloved Duke when I was manically divorcing Scott. Although my dad had Meg's pup, Lil, and another dog from the Appalachian man, Gracie, I thought it would be wonderful to have a loyal and loving dog of my own once again.

I found a breeder in Southern Wisconsin who bred English Pointers and English Setters. He just had a litter ready when I called. I made my journey to his kennel and picked a male. He was black and white, just like Duke. His pedigree was amazing. I named him Bo. He immediately became my favorite companion and buddy. I was so excited to start training and hunting behind him.

I still struggled through my depression, and the heaviness of it weighed on my soul, but I continued to work hard at my job. Meanwhile, my online friendship persisted, despite the complexities inherent in long-distance relationships. Through the spring and into the warm summer months of June, we maintained our connection, finding solace in our conversations.

Family turmoil

In June, I met a guy named Tom at my dad's church in Virginia, MN. He was a good-looking guy, a little older than me. He had a disabled child. I may have been drawn to that, thinking because he has disabled children, he must be a good guy. In July 2011, my family was invited to my relatives on the 4th of July. I invited Tom to my relatives for the 4th. He with my nephews were playing basketball outside. I went to check on them, and my nephew was crying, saying that Tom pushed him.

I said to Tom, *"That's not right."*

His response was, *"He pushed me first."*

"Really!" I thought, *"You're the adult,"* I said. He just smirked.

I went back into the house to check on my nephew, who had run inside crying. I made sure he was ok before I went back outside. One thing led to another, and my brother-in-law Cory and my brother David were fighting outside. I did what I could by jumping on my brother's back to stop the fighting. My one relative even tried stopping the fight. I held my brother tight, trying to stop him while I also prayed.

He didn't stop until Kim, his wife, came out yelling, *"David, stop, that's enough!"*

Kim was nine months pregnant at the time. My sister Jen was upset because Cory could barely talk from the fight. David had a black eye. The police arrived due to the fighting. My dad was upset with my sister Jen regarding the whole deal. It was such a fiasco. We were all so broken and still mourning Mom's death. My mom was the glue that held our family together. The worst for me was riding home with Tom. I should have never invited him for the

4th. I didn't talk the entire drive back home. When I arrived back to drop him off, he wanted to kiss me. I was disgusted and enraged. I said, *"How dare you!"* He said, *"What are you talking about?"*

"Really?" I said, *"You have no idea."*

He just pridefully shrugged and said, "I didn't do anything wrong."

I slugged him on the shoulder and said, *"I never want to see you again, ever."* Tom started the whole fiasco at my relative's place.

Death or a Miracle

The following days are a blur. I do remember my dad was invited to a men's retreat with my brother Greg in Montana. I was at home, alone, depressed, and ready to give up. I just wanted to sleep away life. I never planned to harm myself; I just wanted my old life back. I went to the medicine cabinet to take my prescribed Lithium, Depakote, and PRN Ativan like I always do.

This time, though, I took all the pills left in the bottles and went to bed. Apparently, I called my sister Jen, but I don't remember doing that. She was concerned by what I said and called 911. I remember laying in my bed, and a paramedic came into my room and woke me. I think she checked my vitals and asked if I was ok. *"Fine,"* I said, and she left.

At that point, I decided I wanted to go to my sister Jen's in Duluth. I didn't want to be alone. Mind you, I swallowed all my medication prior to that. I got in my car and drove towards Duluth. I called my dad's pastor. I have no idea what I said, but I know he prayed for me over the phone. The only other thing I remember is the tail lights on a blue car that was in front of me the entire drive to Duluth.

As I pulled up to Jen and Cory's house, Cory hurried outside to assist me, sensing my distress. Despite their concern, I couldn't hold back the nausea, and I vomited right there. Worried about my well-being, they swiftly rushed me to the hospital, but the details were a blur to me. Apparently, I drifted in and out of consciousness, only regaining awareness the following day, clad in a bright yellow gown with a bucket by my side. The medical staff administered activated charcoal, a remedy I vaguely recall.

Coincidentally, my sister-in-law Kim found herself in the same hospital as me. She had been transferred to Duluth due to complications during labor, and while I was undergoing detox, my nephew Chase entered the world.

The most surreal part of this ordeal was the profound transformation that followed. After enduring the depths of depression, undergoing treatment, and spending a night in the hospital, I emerged feeling liberated. It was as though a heavy weight had been lifted, and I rediscovered my true self. I firmly attribute this newfound freedom to the unwavering prayers of my loved ones, which enveloped me in an overwhelming sense of gratitude. Once again, I witnessed the power of prayer as the Lord answered our pleas.

Thankfully, I didn't miss any work since I had a long weekend. When I returned to work, I felt completely refreshed and reinvigorated.

Blessings

In the final week of July, my supervisor approached me with thrilling news. She shared that a supervisory role had become available at another group home and encouraged me to apply, assuring me of her support. Although a bit nervous, I was also filled with excitement at the prospect of advancing in my career. Trusting my supervisor's judgment, I decided to seize the opportunity.

To my joy, I received the promotion promptly and was relocated to a new group home in a different town. The workplace was stunning, offering ample space and a warm atmosphere. I felt invigorated and ready to embrace the fresh challenges and responsibilities that awaited me.

I shared my good news with my online friend Kangas, who had been a great source of support and encouragement since we first started talking. He was happy for me and decided to visit. We spent time drawing together, which was pretty cool. We went fishing for bass; it was the first time I fished bass, and I loved it!

I was so used to fishing walleye with my dad. After seeing how much Kangas liked the area and how well we got along, he made the decision to move here. He rented a spacious apartment in the heart of downtown Chisholm, and we continued to hang out fishing, drawing, and enjoying the great outdoors.

As the warm summer days began to fade, our family was gradually finding ways to navigate life without our beloved mom. Dad had reconnected with an old high school friend, and their conversations brought a sense of comfort and companionship to his otherwise somber days. Meanwhile, I found solace in the presence of my friend Kangas, who had recently moved to town. We shared endless conversations filled with laughter and camaraderie, offering a ray of light in the midst of darkness. Additionally, my job provided me with a sense of purpose and stability, grounding me during this period of adjustment and healing.

David and Kim had just welcomed their first child, baby Chase, into the world, and seeing them dote on him was a heartwarming sight. As for the rest of my siblings, they all seemed to be doing okay, too. It wasn't easy, but we were all trying to move forward while holding onto the memories of our dear mom, whose absence we felt acutely every day.

After spending a few months in my new position, I was approached by the head manager, who informed me about an exciting new role. Intrigued by the opportunity, I followed her advice and applied for the position, and to my delight, I was offered another promotion. With the increase in my income, I felt more financially stable, which inspired me to search for a new home in the winter of 2011.

During my search, I stumbled upon a charming little house in the picturesque countryside that immediately caught my eye. The house exuded warmth and coziness, and it seemed like the perfect fit for my dad and me, who had always talked about moving to the countryside. It was particularly difficult for him to continue living in the house where my mom had passed, so I decided to look for a new home for both of us.

As I guided my dad through the new house, a feeling of joy washed over me. The property boasted over 13 acres of land, enveloped by expansive spruce and birch woods, with a railway line bordering it. While the tracks were seldom used, mainly for transporting taconite pellets and lumber once or twice a week, the occasional train passing by added a quaint touch to the surroundings.

The house itself was a quaint and cozy one-and-a-half-story structure, with a large loft-style bedroom upstairs and a comfortable bedroom on the main floor. The living and dining room, adorned with rustic décor, gave the home a warm and inviting feel. The kitchen, though small, was well-equipped, and the nearby bathroom was neat and tidy. As I showed my dad around, I couldn't help but think that this was the perfect place for us to call home.

After much consideration, my dad decided to sell his old house and move in with me. Our realtor was able to sell his house quickly, and we were both able to sign the necessary paperwork smoothly.

When it came time to clean out my childhood home, which was also my dad's old house, my family came to help. Going through old memories and belongings was both challenging and healing, but with my mom's organized approach, we were able to clear out the house quickly.

"Through prayers of protection from my brothers and sisters in Christ, God's sovereign mercy and grace saved me. Death was not victorious; depression will never win."
Our God is a God of salvation, and a God, the Lord, belongs deliverance from death.- Psalm 68:20

Chapter 15

Rollercoaster Ride of 2012

New Home

For the last two years prior to purchasing the house, I was dealing with gallbladder pain off and on. I tried different diets and fads, but nothing worked. The pain was getting so severe that I could hardly move. Eventually, my doctor said I should get my gallbladder removed, so I had surgery in April 2012. The same month, we cleaned out my dad's house. It was moving day, and I was two days post-surgery, but I didn't care; there was too much to do, so I worked diligently moving everything.

In March, my dad and I decided to breed his beautiful English Pointer, Gracie, with my handsome English Pointer, Bo. The anticipation of the arrival of these new puppies was high, and I was excited to know that I had already pre-sold a couple of them to hunters who were well-known to both my dad and me. As the due date was set for May, I had my work cut out for me. There was so much to do in preparation, and I worked diligently to ensure that everything was in place before their arrival. From getting the whelping box ready to stock up on supplies, I made sure that nothing was left to chance. Kangas was a carpenter, so he made a very nice whelping box for Gracie and her pups. My new home, nestled in the serene countryside, was the perfect place to raise a litter of adorable puppies. On the side of the house, there was a charming brown-painted wooden fence that led to the kitchen and the basement through the door. The fenced yard, adorned with a beautiful white pine tree, is the centerpiece of the outdoor space. The white pine tree is my absolute favorite tree because of its unique and robust nature. Each white pine tree has a distinctive appearance, making it a one-of-a-kind natural wonder. The wispy needles of the white pine rustle in the wind, creating a soothing sound that resonates through through the air.

SCARE

One morning in early May, I received a call from my dad.

"Vicky, I need my nitro pills," he said.

I responded, *"You ok, dad?"*

He just said, *"Bring me my nitro pills."* I know my dad a little too well. He was too stubborn to get help by calling 911, nor would he like it if I called 911. I grabbed his nitro and drove to Hibbing, where he was sitting in his truck, leaning over and resting his arm on the seat. I gave him his nitro.

I said, *"Dad, you should go to the hospital."* He responded by smirking at me.

I said, *"Move over; I'll drive you there."* Even as I drove towards the hospital, which wasn't that far away, he told me how to drive, typical dad.

We arrived at the Emergency Room while they assisted my dad into a wheelchair and set up an EKG. They got him into a bed while hooking him up to evaluate him. The doctor stated, *"Ken, you're having a heart attack."*

My dad looked up at me, tears streaming down his face, saying, *"I'm going home."*

He was crying but happy at the same time. My dad wanted nothing more than to be with Jesus and my mom.

The ER doctor approached me, saying, *"You're really white. Are you pregnant?"*

I looked at her oddly and said, *"My dad is having a heart attack."* She smiled as if to agree and offered me a chair.

Dad's heart attack was so severe that he required further treatment. The emergency department summoned the helicopter response team. My brother David recounted how he watched them load Dad into the helicopter, witnessing their struggle to fit the stretcher inside. They banged the stretcher against the side of the helicopter repeatedly in their efforts. Despite the commotion, David could see Dad laughing at their attempts. Eventually, Dad was flown to Duluth, where doctors inserted three stents in his heart. Prior to Dad having the heart attack, he had minor surgery on his feet to remove bunions. While he was in the hospital for the stints, the doctors noticed he had an infection from the surgery. He was discharged from the hospital, but they made him go to a nursing home temporarily due to the medication pump for the infection.

During this time, he stayed at the Buhl nursing home, but he found it miserable and dull. Longing to return home, I made it a routine to pick him up daily after work, bringing him back home for the afternoon and evening. His days were spent watching the news, reading the Bible and newspaper, and sending text messages containing scripture verses to people, a newfound joy for him. He took pride in his ability to text, even on a flip phone. After a few weeks, he was discharged from the nursing home, and his happiness knew no bounds as he returned home.

Since my mom passed, I noticed that my dad was struggling with various everyday tasks due to his severe arthritis and aging. The condition had taken a toll on his hands, making it challenging for him to perform simple tasks like writing or even opening things. As I watched him struggle, I couldn't help but feel sorry for him, and it reminded me of the days when I was dependent on him to perform similar tasks for me when I was young.

Determined to assist him in any way I could, I stepped in and took over several essential functions for him. I wrote his checks, ordered his medications, and even set up a medication box for him as he was taking several medicines. I wanted to ensure that he received everything he needed and was satisfied with the arrangements, even though he was grumpy at times. Sometimes, I felt like he treated me like he treated my mom when he got upset.

Puppies!

On a beautiful spring day, May 22nd to be exact, I was outside enjoying the warm sun with our three furry companions: Lil, Bo, and Gracie. It was a peaceful afternoon, and we were all lounging in the grass, soaking up the sunshine. Suddenly, Gracie got up and headed towards the house, indicating that she wanted to go back inside. I followed her, and as I opened the door, she rushed inside and headed straight for the basement. I assumed she wanted to cool off, but after about 10 minutes, I began to wonder why she headed for the basement.

I decided to check on her, and as I entered the basement, I was greeted with a sight that filled me with excitement and joy: Gracie was on the basement couch with two adorable puppies already born! I couldn't believe it! It was an unexpected surprise that thrilled me to no end. I couldn't contain my excitement as I hurried upstairs to share the news with my dad before rushing back downstairs to assist Gracie with the rest of her labor.

I moved the two pups to the warm whelping box, and Gracie followed. As I watched her give birth to each of her eight puppies, my heart swelled with love and admiration. She gave birth to six beautiful females and two handsome males, four of whom had black and white fur, and the other four had liver and white fur. The whole experience was truly breathtaking, and I will never forget the moment when Gracie brought eight little miracles into this world.

Concerned, I contacted a vet who visited our home to check her out. The vet suspected dehydration and administered electrolytes to Gracie. However, despite the treatment, Gracie did not show signs of improvement. We sought a second opinion from another veterinarian, who diagnosed her with a pyometra infection in her uterus. It was a serious condition, and Gracie was too weak to care for her puppies or undergo treatment on her own.

I had to break the news to my dad, who owned Gracie, but unfortunately, he couldn't afford the necessary treatment. The vet, seeing the urgency of the situation, offered to cover the cost of the surgery and provide ongoing care for Gracie. However, this also meant that Gracie would have to be surrendered to the vet's care. It was a difficult decision, but ultimately, my dad agreed in the best interest of Gracie's health and well-being.

I wanted to know how Gracie was doing, so I called the vet. The vet stated after surgery, Gracie died. *How sad,* I thought, that disease is horrible. I'm thankful that even though she had pyometra, the puppies were okay.

Taking care of eight newborn puppies was incredibly overwhelming, especially with my dad recovering from heart surgery and battling arthritis. Thankfully, my eleven-year-old nephew Joey stepped up and became my hero during this challenging time. His cheerful and helpful nature was a true blessing as he assisted me with feeding and caring for the puppies, alongside Kangas, who was also a significant help.

Feeding and tending to the puppies every two hours was an arduous task, but our commitment to their health and well-being never wavered. To monitor their progress, I created a tracking sheet and gave each pup a unique name based on their personality and traits. Since they were too young to eliminate on their own, we had to assist them until they were 2 to 3 weeks old, requiring patience and gentle care.

Initially, we fed them store-bought puppy formula, but later, we switched to a homemade recipe provided by a friend. Though making the formula was time-consuming, we took pride in our efforts when we saw how healthy and lively the puppies grew. Despite the challenges, the experience of nurturing the puppies was unforgettable and brought our family closer together.

Balancing full-time work with puppy care was exhausting, but my friend Missy offered to take the puppies for a weekend to give me a much-needed break. I was grateful for her support, especially considering how we had drifted apart during high school and our twenties. Reconnecting with her during this time was a silver lining in the midst of a hectic period.

As the puppies matured, they developed the ability to consume canned dog food mixed with formula, allowing them to feed themselves. Additionally, they were able to relieve themselves without requiring assistance. I felt immense gratitude that they were able to receive the essential colostrum from Gracie, which played a critical role in their early development.

Raising eight playful puppies without their momma, Gracie, presented a unique and heartwarming challenge. However, under the watchful eye of their daddy, Bo, they flourished. Bo proved to be an extraordinary father, lavishing his attention on his little ones with boundless affection and patience.

Throughout the day, Bo engaged in endless play sessions with the puppies, allowing them to clamber over him and nibble on his ears without complaint. His gentle demeanor and unwavering devotion created a nurturing environment in which the puppies thrived.

One particularly memorable moment captured the essence of their bond. In the backyard, amid the towering white pine trees, the puppies frolicked with joy, playing a spirited game of tag. On one side of the tree, Bo patiently awaited their playful advances, his calm presence a reassuring beacon for his curious offspring

peeking around the trunk. Together, they epitomized the beauty of familial love and companionship.

Lil, on the other hand, wanted nothing to do with puppies; she never did. She was an exceptional hunting dog and my mom's favorite, but she had a unique personality. Lil was the runt of the litter from Meg's first litter in 2003. Only a day old, she stopped breathing and became cold in my hands. We thought she had passed away, but my dad came to her rescue. He took her, wrapped her in a towel, and gently rubbed her, and miraculously, Lil started breathing again. For a few days, my dad had to feed her with an eye dropper until she was strong enough to join her siblings. My parents were so attached to her that they decided to keep her and named her 'Nita's Lil Hunter.' Lil grew up to be a loyal companion and a skilled hunting dog.

All the puppies found their new homes, with some staying locally and others traveling out of state. One puppy, in particular, caught the attention of a hunter named Pat and his wife, whom I had met through the Appalachian friends who visited Minnesota for hunting trips. They were seeking a black and white male puppy with a strong hunting drive for extended hunting sessions. Pat hired me to train the pup over the summer until he and his wife arrived in October.

Training English Pointer puppies was always a pleasure for me because they exhibited a natural talent for their craft, and they were usually highly trainable. I looked forward to working with this pup and helping him develop his hunting skills.

Family

In 2012, my niece Sarah graduated from post-secondary college after completing two years of education. She wished to organize a graduation party, so she requested me to host it at my place in the county where her Papa (Kenny) lived, and it was closer to most of our relatives. I was thrilled to accept her request and was looking forward to it.

To make sure we had a contingency plan in case the weather turned bad, Missy generously agreed to lend us a large white tent. Kangas, on the other hand, did everything he could to help prepare the yard with the tent, fire pit, and yard games. My sisters assisted with food preparation to ensure everything was perfect.

The air buzzed with excitement as our extended family, including siblings, aunts, uncles, cousins, and their families, gathered to celebrate Sarah's graduation party. We indulged in a plethora of activities, playing volleyball and yard games, and relished every moment of catching up with each other.

My brother Greg, who extended his stay, spent some quality time with Dad. Together, Dad, Greg, and I ventured out to a local lake for a much-anticipated fishing trip. Though our efforts yielded no catch, the true reward lay in the precious moments shared amidst the serene backdrop. The tranquility of the surroundings, coupled with the warmth of companionship, rendered the experience truly unforgettable.

Throughout the summer after the graduation party, my days were packed with various activities, from working as a manager for group homes to helping my dad and spending time with Kangas. My nephew Joey also spent most of his summer break with us, and we had a great time together.

Hunting

With the anticipation of the fall season, we all looked forward to our annual pheasant hunting trip at a local preserve. One sunny Saturday morning in October, my dad, his friend Michael, his two sons, my brother David and Kangas, my nephew Adel, and I began our journey to the preserve located north of Chisholm. The weather was warmer than usual, and the sun shone bright, casting a golden hue over everything, making the day even more enjoyable. We had three dogs with us: Lil, Bo, and Duke. Duke was always intense when it came to hunting pheasants, and he was incredibly skilled at it. Even though I didn't 'own' Duke anymore, I was thankful my ex-husband Scott let me hunt with him.

As we walked through the field, Dad took charge, saying, "Everyone makes a line while we walk through this field as the dogs work it." The tall grass swayed in the gentle breeze, and we could hear the rustling of the leaves. Suddenly, Lil went on point, and a spooky hen flushed out of a thicket of grass and flew towards the West. In unison, we aimed and fired. 'Bang, bang' down it went. Sometimes, we didn't know who got the bird because a few of us would shoot at the same time. I will admit, I never figured I got it. I wasn't the best shot, especially to my right.

As we divided into smaller groups, each accompanied by a skilled hunting dog, anticipation filled the crisp autumn air. Adel, David, and Kangas, seasoned hunters in their own right, seldom failed to hit their mark. Michael's son, too, displayed remarkable accuracy, seemingly never missing a shot. Together, fueled by determination and camaraderie, we embarked on our hunt.

Throughout the day, our efforts yielded unprecedented success. With precision and teamwork, we managed to bring down all 30 birds we had set out to hunt—an achievement that surpassed our previous endeavors. In years past, we had typically acquired 20-30 birds, yet never had we succeeded in bagging them all. This year, however, was different. Our persistence paid off, and as we gathered our spoils, a sense of pride washed over us, underscoring the significance of our accomplishment.

Overall, it was a fantastic day, and we had a great time bonding over our shared love for pheasant hunting. We shared many laughs and jokes while walking and hunting. As the sun began to set, we packed up our gear and headed back home, tired but exhilarated. These memories will always hold a special place in my heart. Each year, Dad, my brother David, myself, and a group of others went pheasant hunting. And every year, we created new memories and laughed at the same old jokes.

Stressful times

As November rolled in, my workplace became a stressful environment. A couple of my staff members were out sick, and one of them was responsible for the overnight shift. Unfortunately, no one else was available to cover for them. As a result, I had to take on the extra work and work the overnight shifts myself, in addition to carrying out my usual duties. It was a challenging time for me.

I put in long, grueling hours for weeks, working day and night. Unfortunately, some employees make things even more difficult. It's tough to manage people in any field, but working in social services can be particularly draining. The emotional weight of the job, coupled with the added stress of managing difficult staff, really took its toll on me.

Deer Hunting

During this time, my dad found solace in the familiar routine of visiting a local restaurant, where he'd spend his days sipping coffee and reminiscing about days gone by with fellow patrons. In the afternoons, he'd indulge in watching the news and preparing some of his favorite meals, like Italian beef roast and skillet spaghetti. Ensuring his comfort remained a priority for me, from managing his bills to ensuring he had an ample supply of medications. Despite his health challenges, my dad's love for deer hunting persisted. While he could no longer manage certain tasks, such as driving deer to each person in the stand, we were fortunate to secure hunting permission on a property north of Chisholm, thanks to a friend. Fondly recalling the lease agreement, my dad would jest,

"I paid the lease with mom's blueberry pie." Over the years, my brother-in-law Cory and others had worked to clear trails, making them more accessible for hunters like my dad.

In the hunting season of 2012, my dad's persistence paid off, as he proudly harvested four deer. A snapshot captured him leaning on a 4-wheeler next to two of the deer, a moment of accomplishment and pride that brought joy to him and our family.

My dad, Kenny, and I – Pheasant hunt

Hunter's end

As Thanksgiving approached, our family was cordially invited to Jen and Cory's house, and we spent a pleasant evening together. Since it was Thanksgiving break, my nephew Joey was invited to stay with us. Over Thanksgiving weekend, I took care of a lady's horses who lived a few miles away. On Friday night, my dad mentioned to me that he would be going to bed early as he was planning to check trap lines with his friend Joe and my uncle early in the morning. I did not worry as this was a typical activity for him, and he would be going with a friend.

Saturday morning, I was feeding the horses I was taking care of when my phone rang. My phone showed, 'Dad calling.'

I answered jokingly, *"What up, ol' man?"*

But instead, it was Joe on the other end saying, *"Vicky, I am so sorry, your dad is gone."*

I didn't say anything at first; I then said, *"What do you mean?"*

Joe responded with, *"Vicky, I tried to help him, but he died."*

I immediately tried calling my siblings. I got a hold of Roseann, and she responded by crying and screaming. I attempted to reach Jen and got a hold of Cory. I asked Cory to please start calling everyone. As I drove back to my house, all I could think about was Joey. How was I going to tell him Papa had passed away? I called Kangas, and he immediately left work to be with us. I walked into my house, sat down by Joey, and said, *"Papa is in heaven with Nanny."* It was one of the hardest things I ever had to say to a kid.

My dad, Joe, and my uncle were on the Echo Trail 40 miles away from Orr, Minnesota. My dad had a massive heart attack in the woods while he was reaching for his nitro pills in the truck. I felt so bad for my uncle and Joe—no phone service. Joe had to drive with my dad passed away into Orr, to call 911. It was November 24th, 2012.

After my dad had a heart attack in May, I prayed, *"Lord, please don't let me find my dad dead at home."*

I couldn't bear the idea of finding my dad passed away in bed when I woke up or when I got home from work. I would call him a couple of times a day while I was at work to see how he was doing. When he wouldn't answer, I would ask someone like Missy to go check on him.

He would tease me afterward, saying, *"You having someone check on me to see if I died?"* He was such a bear.

It was a bittersweet moment when my dad passed away, doing what he loved most—surrounded by the vast beauty of God's wilderness alongside cherished friends. His love for the outdoors was profound, and it was fitting that he departed from a place that brought him immense joy and peace. Remarkably, it was in the same region where he had his first heart attack 24 years earlier, a testament to his enduring spirit and passion for the woods.

As Joe shared the details of my dad's final moments, mentioning the fisher in the trap he was checking, I couldn't help but feel a mix of emotions. Over the years, my dad had encountered numerous close calls with death, perhaps preparing me in some way for the inevitable. Yet, despite this preparation, the loss was profound, and I found myself grieving deeply for my dad, my hunting companion, and the pillar of our family. His absence left a void that could never be filled, and I missed him dearly with each passing day.

That year, Christmas felt different. It was a time when families came together, but my family didn't plan anything. We were all still trying to cope with the loss of Dad. Instead, I spent Christmas with Kangas's family. It was a heartwarming experience. His parents welcomed me with open arms and treated me like one of their own. Kangas's sister, along with her kids, made the day even more special. We played board games, ate delicious food, and shared stories. It was a pleasant and comforting break from the grief that had consumed me for weeks.

"Even though I lost my dad, I held his memory strongly in my heart. He was my confidant who taught me so much about the outdoors and God's fervent hand. I saw him as a good father figure regardless of his flaws. This year marked many changes and occurrences in my life that stay close to my strongest memories."

Train a child in the way he should go, and when he is old, he shall not turn from it. -Proverbs 22:6

Chapter 16

2013 - 2014

Stable

Despite enduring numerous hardships over the past year, I found myself somewhat taken aback by the stability of my mental health—or so I believed. Considering the upheaval stemming from the loss of my mom, the subsequent divorce, and bouts of mania and depression that led to hospitalizations, I felt a deep sense of gratitude for simply managing to hold it together after the loss of my dad. Given my history, characterized by recurrent manic episodes triggered by stress, it was a welcome surprise to find myself faring relatively well. Reflecting on the frequency of my hospitalizations for mental health issues—spanning from 1992, 1995, 1996 three times, 1998 two times, 2001 two times, 2004, 2006, 2010 two times, to 2011. That's a lot, in my opinion, for mental health hospitalizations.

A time of change

The next year arrived swiftly, and I felt a sudden urge to visit my brother Greg in Illinois. So, Kangas and I embarked on a road trip there in May. It was a delightful experience as Greg graciously showed us around many of Chicago's landmarks. Life appeared to settle into a rhythm. Kangas moved in to help me manage living expenses following my dad's passing, despite my usual reluctance to share living space with a man. Kangas, being a skilled handyman and carpenter, adeptly addressed any household repairs and even upgraded the basement's water tubing, enhancing its functionality. Together, we refreshed the kitchen with a new coat of paint. Although life seemed relatively stable, we grappled with our individual challenges and didn't always see eye to eye.

Nonetheless, I was eager to welcome a horse into my life. A former acquaintance with whom I used to babysit and ride horses expressed interest in boarding her horse. Kangas constructed a lean-to attached to the small barn, while I worked on building a fence. Before long, my property was horse-ready.

In July 2013, I came across Charlie, a 12-year-old gray quarter horse—a color I had a fondness for. While not as graceful as my old horse Spirit, Charlie had a certain charm that reminded me of him. Meanwhile, the acquaintance found a suitable companion for Charlie in a pony named Billy. We enjoyed riding in the area and exploring nearby trails.

Despite our differences, Kangas and I still engaged in enjoyable activities like fishing at Pelican Lake or Side Lake, grouse hunting, and creating artwork together. One memorable hunting excursion involved my sister Jen joining us for a pheasant hunt. Additionally, I was commissioned to draw a portrait of a dog named Rock, a descendant of a litter I had bred, while Kangas contributed his artistic touch to the piece.

We made the most of the summer by fishing as often as possible, even exploring a small lake within walking distance from home. While we caught plenty of Northern Pike, we opted not to keep them for consumption, relishing the thrill of the catch. I couldn't help but miss fishing with my dad, whose wisdom and knowledge of fishing spots were sorely missed.

Come fall, Kangas and I found ourselves hunting in Dad's old hunting grounds along the wolf trail. A heartwarming moment ensued when Kangas, initially believing he had missed a shot, was pleasantly surprised as Lil, Dad's faithful dog, retrieved the bird he thought he had lost. Moved by Lil's efforts, Kangas couldn't contain his joy.

In October, we honored Dad's memory with a pheasant hunt, joined by family members and friends. As we reminisced about Dad's hunting stories, we each bagged our fair share of pheasants, creating lasting memories in his honor.

Shortly after the hunting season, Kangas and I decided to part ways. Our relationship had run its course, and I found it increasingly challenging to sustain.

Kelly

While attending church in Hibbing, I had the pleasure of meeting Kelly, a vibrant and energetic 19-year-old girl. From our first encounter, we hit it off and quickly became close friends, despite our age gap. Our friendship blossomed, and our bond

182

flourished due to our shared passions for photography, agates, poetry, lighthearted laughter, the outdoors, and, above all, our faith in Jesus.

We would often spend hours discussing different topics, ranging from the Bible to our favorite poetry. What I appreciated most about her was how she made me feel comfortable in her presence, allowing me to be myself. Perhaps it's because she reminds me of my younger self. Whatever the reason, our friendship continued to grow stronger over time. Kelly is an amazing woman of God, and I feel incredibly blessed to have her in my life. She remained steadfast and kind to me even during a manic episode I experienced.

Kelly moved to California, and married a wonderful young man. She lived there for seven years before returning to Minnesota. During the time Kelly lived in California, our friendship remained, but we didn't stay in touch. After she moved back to Minnesota with her husband in 2022, our friendship blossomed again, regardless of the fact we live in different parts of the state. Kelly is an amazing woman that I cherish deeply. She's such a dear friend with a huge heart.

2014

On a peaceful Friday evening, I received a kind invitation from an acquaintance to attend a church service. As the worship began, the melodious sound of the drums drew my attention. The drummer was in full flow, and his beats were in perfect harmony with the music. Our eyes briefly met, sparking a momentary connection that caused me to shy away. Yet, I found myself repeatedly drawn to him throughout the service.

As the service progressed, I saw him sitting next to Jean, a lady I knew from my parent's church, who was always hospitable and inviting. Following the service, Jean introduced me to her son, Terry, who happened to be the talented drummer I had admired earlier. As we engaged in conversation, I was captivated by Terry's love for music and his unwavering faith.

I started attending his church in a small northeastern town, where I was struck by the beauty of the praise and worship and the warmth of the congregation. The praise and worship deeply honored Jesus, which touched me deeply. After the service, Terry and I spent time together, sharing laughter and meaningful conversations. I found myself eagerly anticipating these moments with each passing week.

Oh, my heart

One November evening, while I was engrossed in reading the Bible and praying, I suddenly experienced a sharp pain shooting through my left jaw and arm. Simultaneously, my chest began to ache, prompting concern. I promptly reached out to my neighbor, who resided across the road, and she promptly dialed 911. In addition, I contacted Terry, the drummer, my dearest friend.

Paramedics arrived and checked my vitals. My blood pressure read 220/170, so they gave me nitro and morphine for my chest pain and completed an EKG while they brought me to the ER. One of the paramedics interpreted the EKG results, indicating it resembled a heart attack. It seemed implausible for someone as young as me, merely 37 years old, to be experiencing a potential heart attack.

During my time in the emergency room, despite persistent high blood pressure, the doctor concluded that I had not suffered a heart attack. Terry came to the ER. He arrived after midnight. Once they stabilized my blood pressure, they sent me home and asked me to visit my primary doctor.

Subsequently, I encountered a couple more instances of excruciatingly high blood pressure and pain, prompting my doctor to order a stress echocardiogram. Surprisingly, the results came back normal. Interestingly, the women I attended Bible study with prayed over me, and my siblings also offered their prayers. I firmly believe that the power of prayer played a role in healing whatever ailment had affected my heart. Some speculate that it was an attack orchestrated by the devil, as he perpetually seeks to undermine us.

"During this phase of my life, I developed a great deal of self-sufficiency and maintained a consistent lifestyle. Moreover, I forged fresh and significant connections with like-minded Christians."

Encourage one another and build each other up, just as, in fact, you are doing. - 1 Thessalonians 5:11

Chapter 17

Healed?

He is faithful

As I walked through the door of my home on August 14th, I felt a sense of relief after a busy day at work. I immediately went to my music collection and selected some of my favorite tunes. I decided to spend some time worshiping the Lord, as it always brings me a sense of calm and peace. While singing along to a praise song, I couldn't help but be encouraged by the lyrics.

They reminded me of the powerful words a visiting minister shared at church, *"You are holy, blameless and without accusation,"* from the scripture Colossians 1:22. These words deeply resonated with me as I felt a sense of gratitude and appreciation for my faith.

As the song 'He is Faithful' started, I thought I felt the Holy Spirit moving, and I began to press in and pray earnestly. I then heard in that still, small voice, *"You are healed, you are blameless, without accusation, you are delivered and free, you don't need your medications anymore."*

For as long as I have dealt with bipolar, that's all I've ever wanted! I wanted to be *'normal'* and not have to deal with this deliberating disease. I longed for an escape from an illness that had repeatedly wreaked havoc on my life. It brought about setbacks, severed friendships, cost me jobs, dissolved my marriage, plunged me into debt, led me into risky encounters, fueled reckless behavior behind the wheel, and inflicted harm through erratic speech and actions. All I ever wanted was to be free. I cried so many tears, prayed so many times, sought prayer from elders in churches, been prayed over by church leaders and family, and tried different diets, but nothing ever worked.

I nearly died from driving without sleep for days and ended up in the ditch. I drove on recklessly and up steep iron ore trails and ruined my car. I took all my medication and could have died either driving while overdosed or dying from the overdose. I could have been hurt or killed by some of these men I was with while in a manic state. Countless things could have ended my life. So, hearing in my spirit, *"You are healed,"* my heart leaped for joy; I truly wanted to believe it. I shared it with some family and close friends I trusted, and they were encouraged by it. Only one person tested what I heard: my brother Greg. He said, *"Maybe God healed your heart (emotion), but it would be good to still take your medication."*

But I felt I was ok. I have had no symptoms or issues with depression since July 2011 and mania since 2010. It was 2014, after all; that was a record for me, no episodes of bipolar for four years. This *'word'* in my spirit had to be true.

I confidently stopped taking my Depakote and Lithium medication, and everything seemed to be going well.

Friends Gathering

The holiday season was upon us, and I couldn't wait to host a gathering with my dear friends from church. I had invited a group of wonderful people including Kelly, most of whom were younger than me, to come to my place. Whether we attended Friday night prayer sessions or worship services together, our connection ran deep.

When Christmas day finally arrived, I put my cooking skills to the test and prepared rigatoni for everyone, using my dad's recipe. The sauce, brimming with wild game such as grouse harvested earlier that season, filled the air with its irresistible aroma. Laughter resonated throughout the house as we savored every delicious bite, accompanied by delectable chocolate bars and engaging games that kept us entertained well into the night. It was a memorable evening, overflowing with joy and warmth.

As the New Year approached, we were all excited to celebrate it together. New Year's Eve unfolded with a delightful mix of goofiness and laughter, as we engaged in games, attempted to form a human pyramid, and shared our aspirations for the upcoming year. The spirit of camaraderie enveloped us, and the cherished memories forged that night will forever hold a special place in our hearts.

A shift

I found myself in need of a respite from the whirlwind of my daily life. Juggling work commitments, household chores, social engagements, church activities, and spending cherished moments with my close friend Terry left me feeling drained and weary. So, I decided to plan a vacation to Cumberland Gap, the place where I retreated to when my mom passed away. I booked a stay at a bed and breakfast and headed there over my birthday in April.

During the drive, I stopped at a hotel halfway to rest. However, despite my best efforts, sleep eluded me both at the hotel and during my time in the Gap. I visited a few old friends in the area, but apart from that, I only don't remember a little about the trip.

I am still piecing together how I managed to return home from Cumberland Gap. I recall engaging in behaviors that might be deemed unusual, like discarding my driver's license. I spoke quickly, but I didn't realize that I was not behaving like my usual self, and no one else seemed to notice it either. The only ones who sensed that something was amiss were my family, but with my parents deceased and my siblings relocated from the Iron Range, there were few people in my life who would have detected any anomalies in my behavior.

Upon my arrival home, I felt an overwhelming urge to sell my house and relocate to Virginia, Minnesota. I thought I didn't need my house and could live a simple life. After an extensive search, I found an apartment located in the heart of downtown Virginia that shared bathrooms with other apartments.

The prospect of dwelling in a bustling urban environment thrilled me, although I questioned whether this decision truly reflected my authentic self. Why was I compelled to part with my home?

In preparation for my move, I held a massive garage sale where I sold off numerous items—sold many items, simplifying my life. That's what I should do.

In the spring of 2015, I made some hasty decisions that I regret now. I sold my horse Charlie to a lady in Duluth, MN, without giving it much thought. Unfortunately, my dad's dog, Lil was old and not doing well, so I had to put her down. Later, I received an email from a couple in North Dakota who were looking for a young and trained English Pointer for bird hunting. Since they were interested in a dog like Bo, my beloved English Pointer, I sold him to them. Bo was not only an excellent hunting dog but also my best buddy. After putting Lil down, Terry helped me bury her on my property. Looking back, I realize that I let go of too much too soon. To this day, I miss Bo, he was an amazing dog.

In May, I attended the same church as Terry, a place I had been frequenting for some time. During the service, something within me stirred, and I suddenly felt compelled to leave. I also said some terrible things to Terry and others that were not

194something I would typically say. I don't even want to repeat them; I also don't recall everything I said.

Regrettably, I bid farewell to Terry in a less-than-kind manner, prompting a compassionate church member to offer me refuge in her home upon noticing my evident distress. Despite her gracious gesture, I found it difficult to quiet my restless mind and find solace. Instead, I succumbed to the compulsion to return home and prepare for my impending relocation, as I had sold my house and needed to vacate it by June 1st.

"I still find myself curious about this brief moment in my life. Sometimes, I wonder what would have happened if I had stayed on my medication and ignored the idea of 'being healed.' However, I don't dwell on the past; I choose to learn from it."

The way of the fool is right in his own eyes, but a wise man is he who listens to counsel. -Proverbs 12:15

Beloved, do not believe every spirit but test the spirits to see whether they are from God, for many false prophets have gone out into the world. - 1 John 4:1

Chapter 18

Tailspin

Sam

While exploring downtown Hibbing, I stumbled upon a cozy coffee shop where I met a lovely girl. We hit it off instantly, and I felt a spark of energy within me. Little did I know, that I was experiencing a state of hypomania, though I was oblivious to it at the time. The girl extended an invitation to join her for karaoke at a nearby bar, and I eagerly accepted. We sang our hearts out, and she introduced me to her friend Sam. Sam was a lanky fellow with raven-black hair and a warm demeanor. We all had a fantastic time, singing and having fun. Following the karaoke session, Sam showcased his musical talent by strumming his guitar, leaving me thoroughly impressed.

Sam and I continued to hang out, and he even offered to help me pack my belongings. Despite his efforts, I found myself needing additional help to organize and pack my possessions.

On the day when the new family was moving into my house, I was almost done with the moving process. However, there was one large box of dishes that remained to be transferred, so I just left it in the kitchen. I decided to move most of my items to the workshop in the garage. Before going, I asked the new owner if I could leave my remaining belongings there for a few weeks since   she owed me money for the propane in the tank. She agreed, and we formalized the arrangement by signing a document. My garage now housed a collection of art supplies, artwork, clothing, footwear, kitchenware, decorations, horse tack, and various other items. I assured her that I would retrieve my belongings promptly.

As I settled into my rented apartment, I realized that my furnishings were minimal, consisting only of a bed, an art table, and a chair. In a seemingly spontaneous decision, I opted to relocate a few boxes containing family photos and framed artwork to Sam's father's residence. Though the reasoning behind this choice eluded me, it felt logical at the time.

Let's take a trip!

To celebrate the sale of my house, I invited Sam to come with me to one of my favorite places. I packed my SUV with random clothes, makeup, my computer, an expensive camera, and my dad's rifle. Sam only brought what he was wearing, nothing else.

We started our venture towards a favorite place of mine, Cumberland Gap in Tennessee, with me behind the wheel while Sam was resting. However, I couldn't help but notice his deteriorating condition. He appeared visibly unwell, trembling, shivering, and intermittently drifting off to sleep while expressing discomfort.

Nevertheless, I played my favorite music at full volume, singing and enjoying myself. Every time we stopped at gas stations to refuel, I would get some snacks for us to munch on, but Sam never ate. It's only after looking back that I came to know that he was possibly going through withdrawals.

In my boredom and craziness, while driving, I would call my family, such as my sister-in-law Kim, to share my exciting journey. I only recall a little of this conversation. Kim informed me years later that I was so excited to tell her that my siblings and I were going to start a piccolo band. I said, *"Guess what, Kim! I'm going to play piccolo, Greg can play piano, Jen can sing, David will play guitar, and Rose can sing too!"* I don't remember saying this, but I'm sure I did!

Before heading to Cumberland Gap, I felt it was important to visit my friend Tara. On a beautiful sunny morning in June, my friend Sam and I arrived in the charming Lee County, Virginia, eager to reunite with Tara and John. Upon knocking on their door, we were met with silence, prompting us to explore the horse pasture adjacent to their property, which Tara and John owned. As the sun began to rise, casting a golden hue over the tranquil landscape, we made our way through the grassy hillside toward the grazing horses.

Drawn to the majestic animals, I couldn't resist engaging with them, eliciting playful antics as I made silly noises and gestures, which made the horses run around wildly. Sam, however, found a cozy spot under a tree and dozed off in the shade. Suddenly, I heard footsteps approaching us. It was John, Tara's husband. He looked puzzled and somewhat annoyed at the sight of two strangers in his pasture. His piercing stare made me feel uneasy as he approached us. I greeted him with a smile, saying, *"Good morning, John, so good to see you!"* hoping to ease the tension, but John's furrowed brow betrayed his true feelings. He seemed unimpressed with our presence, and his body language showed it.

Despite my attempts at conversation, John remained silent, his expression one of confusion and disapproval. Undeterred, I continued to chat nervously about our journey and excitement to be there. It wasn't until I inquired about gasoline that John finally responded, breaking the uncomfortable silence between us.

I said, *"John, we are bone dry. Is there any way you have a gas can to give us and a little gas to get to town?"*

He said, *"No, please leave."*

I looked over at Sam and said, *"Well, here we go! Let's go for it. There should be enough of a hill to get us at least to the station in the Gap."*

We navigated our way along the narrow roadway that led to Tara and John's home, eventually reaching Highway 58 in Virginia, which merged with 25E, leading us toward Tennessee and Kentucky. A short drive later, we arrived at the gas station located at the entrance to Cumberland Gap

Selfie while manic June 2015 at a gas station somewhere in Illinois while I was heading to Cumberland Gap

The Gap to crazy town

I was ecstatic to show Sam around one of my favorite towns, Cumberland Gap. Driving down the winding road into the

Gap, nestled among the breathtaking Appalachian Mountains and steeped in rich history, we soaked in the picturesque views. We spent the day exploring every corner of the town, from its quaint stores to the apartment building where I once resided. We even had the opportunity to reconnect with my old friend and former boss at the Frame Shop. After indulging in a delicious meal at a local restaurant, we relaxed in the park and fantasized about making a movie together, my idea, of course. Looking back, I don't know why, but at the time, it seemed like the most fun thing in the world, and we were both eager to make it happen. Crazy, my world seemed normal to me.

Later, as we strolled towards the creek, I ventured onto the trail to observe the overlook and historical markers. However, the scorching heat of that Tuesday made it unbearable. So, we decided to cool off by wading into Cumberland Gap Creek, which flowed directly from the mountain.

Sam noticed a few trout swimming in the creek and said, *"Watch this."* He looked like a true hillbilly with his skinny physique, messy hair, buck teeth, and shirtless while wearing suspenders. He tried to catch one of the trout by repeatedly going underwater or gingerly grabbing for it. Eventually, he succeeded in catching one and tightly grasped it, holding it like a giant teddy bear. The trout squirmed and thrashed its tail in an attempt to break free.

Suddenly, a passerby said, *"Didn't you see the sign??? NO Fishing!"*

We just laughed, thinking, what are the chances of a trout being here in the Gap? Later, we found out that there was terrible flooding early that spring, and that's why the trout were trapped in the creek. Since we had caught the trophy fish, we decided to keep it. Sam stuffed it in a pair of his pants until we could get it on ice. I was elated to tell the story of the trophy trout he caught, and I figured everyone would want to know. We put the fish that was stuffed in a pair of his pants on the back seat of the car, thinking we could get ice.

As the day grew late, we made our way to Middlesboro, Kentucky, just a short distance from Cumberland Gap. Driving up a winding, hilly road and then through the famous mile-long tunnel into Kentucky, we arrived in Middlesboro. This flat city offered various amenities, including dining, shopping, and accommodations. After a brief drive through town, we settled on the Holiday Inn Express for the night.

Whenever we needed anything during our trip, I had been using my card to pay for it. But this time, I gave Sam cash and asked him to put his room in his name. The hotel was a peaceful and pleasant place to stay. My plan for the following day was to head back to Cumberland Gap, Tennessee, and write the movie we had been discussing while relaxing in the Gap.

After indulging in a long, hot bath, I drifted off to sleep. Reflecting on it now, I realized that hot baths were the only thing that seemed to help me sleep, even if only for a short while. The following morning, as I began packing and loading up the car, I noticed that Sam was nowhere to be found. I checked his room, the hallways, and the front desk, but there was no sign of him. Despite trying to reach him by phone, there was no response.

I went back to the room one last time. Sam showed up in a panic, whispering, *"They're here!"*

Shocked, I said, *"Who?"*

He said, *"The cops."*

"So, who cares," I said.

He whispered, *"I gotta go,"* and rushed out of the room.

I couldn't keep up and lost him in the hotel. I went outside looking for him. I did see a police officer walking near the side of Arby's next to the hotel. I approached him, and he just glared at me and sternly said, *"We are here to protect the community."*

"Oookkkkaaaaayyyyyy," I thought and went to my car. I didn't know anything, nor did I understand why Sam was hiding from the police. I got in my vehicle. I didn't realize where Sam was. My phone started ringing, and it was Sam. Frantically, he whispered, *"I'm nowhere near,"* And kept repeating, *"cars"* and *"shop."*

I looked around, puzzled by his statement. He then whispered, *"Walmart."*

Across the highway sat Walmart and other stores, including an auto repair shop. I quietly said, *"I'll come get you."*

I wasn't entirely sure of his whereabouts, but I was determined to find him. Pulling into the auto shop, I parked beside an empty space, with another vehicle adjacent to it. Spotting him emerging from some nearby bushes to the right of that car, I stepped out of my vehicle to greet him.

As I went to greet him, I heard, *"GET DOWN!!!"*

Next thing, Sam is being pushed to the ground by one police officer in front of me. My instinctive reaction was to turn around and observe, only to find another officer aiming a gun directly at me. Extremely frightened, I put my hands in the air with my phone gripped tightly in my hand, turning ghostly white. They were after him for some reason, and I was in the middle of it.

Suddenly, the second officer seized me, forcefully throwing me onto the hood of their police car, causing my phone to slip from my grasp as my knee awkwardly banged against the fender. I was handcuffed and placed in the squad car. They put Sam in the same squad car, and we were hauled together to the station. Sam smirked at me as he squirmed around, causing his hands to go from behind his back to in front of him.

Once at the station, we were confined together in a jail cell, an experience that struck me as peculiar and unconventional. To cope with the tension, I found myself singing and humming songs, perhaps as a means of maintaining some semblance of normalcy amidst the chaos. However, my knee began to throb with pain, likely a result of the rough handling by the officers. Concerned about my injury, I informed them of the discomfort, prompting them to escort me to the hospital for an x-ray, which yielded no significant findings. Upon my return to the jail, I discovered that Sam had been taken elsewhere, presumably booked and placed in a separate cell.

They helped me walk to the booking counter, where a woman working said, *"Pay $45, and here's your disorderly conduct ticket." Really?"* I thought.

"Here's $50, and keep the change," I said.

I asked about my car. I think they said something about Joe's towing, but honestly couldn't understand anything very well with that Appalachian accent. I still could barely walk, so they looked in a closet, gave me this old, worn-out wooden cane, and sent me on my way.

"This experience feels like a strange dream, and I struggle to find the right words to describe it."

Think over what I say, for the Lord will give you understanding.- 2 Timothy 2:7

Chapter 19

How Will I Walk?

Acts of kindness

Day one in the South had been pleasant, but day two took a turn for the worse. It was June 17th, 2015, and barely able to walk, I found myself sitting outside the jail in Pineville. Though I still had my phone and purse, my car was nowhere to be seen. Instead of reaching out for help, I remained seated, lost in my thoughts.

Two compassionate ladies noticed me from across the street and approached, concerned about my well-being. Seeing me sitting on the ground with a cane, they offered me a ride. Gratefully, I accepted, asking to be taken to Middlesboro. I likely rambled on during the journey, but I can't recall what I said or much about that moment. They dropped me off at the Nursing home in town, a place I was familiar with from my past employment in 2010.

Inside the nursing home, I sought refuge near the entrance, feeling utterly exhausted. However, my respite was short-lived as the police arrived and escorted me out, insisting that I leave the premises. Feeling lost and unsure of where to turn, I began to limp away from the nursing home. Why didn't I reach out to those who loved and knew me? Instead, I walked aimlessly until a kind-hearted police officer stopped and offered me a ride, albeit only to the nearby KFC, about 4 miles away. During the ride, I overheard him talking on the phone about his aspirations to become a pastor. It warmed my heart to be helped by a Christian police officer. Upon reaching the KFC, he offered a prayer for me before bidding me farewell. That encounter left a lasting impression on me, and I wished all police officers were as compassionate and understanding as he was.

It was nighttime, and although KFC was closed, I noticed that the Dairy Queen across the street was still open; it was probably around 9 pm. The KFC, Dairy Queen, and a few other businesses were situated at a bustling intersection that led to the mile-long tunnel. I started to carefully hobble across the huge intersection, thinking I would never make it across.

Suddenly, a younger guy riding a bike, who was bandaged up, stopped and said, *"I'll help you."*

Gratefully, I accepted his help, as I was unsure how I would manage to navigate the busy road alone. He grabbed my arm and helped me walk more quickly across the highway. As we reached the other side, a young couple was walking on the sidewalk.

As I am a friendly person who enjoys talking to people, especially when I am manic, I started a conversation with the young couple. It turned out that they were practically homeless and living in poverty, which is unfortunately common in this area.

In response, I offered, *"Let's all go to DQ, I'll buy you all some food, and you can pick!"* The bandaged guy stated he had been hit by a car earlier that day, and he had just left the hospital

His head and left arm were bandaged. I thought, *"Can you believe that! Hit by a car and discharged right away."*

All of us went outside to enjoy the hot summer night to eat our hot food and sweet ice cream. I turned to the young couple nearby and asked if they knew where Joe's towing was located.

They responded with a smile, *"Yes, it's just down the street."*

Grateful for their assistance, I then asked if they could please retrieve my car for me. I had my spare keys in my purse, so I handed the keys to them.

Reflecting on that moment, I can't help but ponder why I had placed my trust in complete strangers with such a crucial task. I recognize now that it's something I would only consider doing in a manic state of mind, and I was not thinking clearly at the time.

Now, while they were gone, I sat there with the bandaged guy who was beginning to pass out and droll. I prayed over him and asked God to help him. When they returned, he snapped out of it and appeared to be ok. They came back within half an hour, stating, *"The owner came out yelling, what the hell you doing! You can't take the car."* The police and the owner of Joe's Towing showed up at the Dairy Queen. I felt like we were gonna get shot, or it felt like we were in a movie where there was a drug bust. None of us moved. I was scared and didn't know what to do. The young couple said to the police, *"We're sorry we made a mistake."*

The police said, *"Don't ever do that again,"* and left with the owner of the towing company.

I asked the young couple and the bandaged guy if anyone had money to help me get my car out. The guy with bandages said that he had some money. As I started counting my cash, he began chatting with the young couple. Unfortunately, I didn't have enough money to pay for getting my car. I couldn't walk to the nearest ATM either, so I asked the young couple if they could withdraw cash from my account. I trusted them to do it for me.

To my surprise, they returned and even provided the receipt. However, they had only checked my checking account, which was empty. Had they examined my savings account, there would have been enough funds available.

"I used to be gullible and fell for tricks quickly, but my desire to help others in need made me an easy target. The state of mind didn't help matters either. I can't believe I gave them my spare keys and debit card, and they brought them back!"

Thus says the Lord, Cursed is the man who trusts in mankind and makes flesh his strength, and whose heart turns away from the Lord.- Jeremiah 17:9

Chapter 20

Darkness

Alone and afraid

That was it - I didn't have any cash to pay for my car. I noticed the man with bandages on his head riding away on his bike. When I looked at the table, I realized my purse was gone. He had stolen it, and it contained my wallet, ID, phone, and debit card - everything I had left. I panicked and yelled; the young couple tried to catch him, but were unable. They didn't come back either. I felt an overwhelming sense of fear that consumed my soul. I was all alone. I sat there, paralyzed by fear, unable to move from the table. The only sound I could hear was the occasional semi-truck passing by on the highway.

The street lights were shimmering in amber hues, but darkness enveloped me. I knew I needed to do something, but I had nothing, just the clothes on my back. I was determined to take some action, so I tried to stand up and walk toward the street light, but my knee kept buckling, and I couldn't move. So, I sat on the ground and dragged myself backward on the sidewalk, just like when I was a baby, backward crawling.

I noticed a semi-truck parked in the lot next to the Dairy Queen. I hoped someone inside could help me, so I crawled backward until I reached the semi and pulled myself up on the rig. I knocked on the truck's window repeatedly, but whoever was inside only waved their hand as if telling me to go away. Disappointed, I got off the semi and continued to drag myself down the sidewalk. As I went, I spotted a huge Baptist church across the street and thought maybe someone there could help me in the morning. I made my way to the church's giant cement steps and carefully dragged myself up each one until I reached the top step. All I wanted to do was sleep, oh, if I could sleep.

As I sat there, leaning against the large red brick, a wave of strong emotions enveloped me, and tears streamed down my cheeks as I thought about Minnesota, my siblings, and my mom and dad. Tears fell as I continued to cry quietly. Wiping away the tears, I looked up and noticed a black car slowly driving across the street from the church with the headlights facing me. The engine and lights turned off. A person got out, stood next to the black car, and just watched me. My heart pounded, and my body froze in place like a scared pup.

Was this the moment? Would there be violence? Would I meet my end? As another vehicle arrived, its spotlight focused on me; I feared the worst. Unsure of what to do, I remained frozen in place, desperately trying to suppress any sound or movement.

They walked up the steps, One rudely saying, *"You can't be here on these steps."*

They were so mean, snide, ugly police officers. No empathy, nothing. I explained how my knee was injured. Nothing.

They grabbed my arms and said, *"Get up, let's go."*

I shared how my dad was a police officer at one time, but they didn't even respond. I tried to explain my situation, but they just cut me off.

One of them said, *"Be quiet, get in; we need to take you somewhere."*

Here I was, back in a squad car again.

I asked, *"Can you bring me to Cumberland Gap?"* Sure enough, they did.

Through the tunnel, we went down the hill to the Gap. They dropped me off at the first corner of the entrance to the Gap.

That night was one of the scariest I have ever encountered. I'm not sure if it was paranoia or actual fear, but I can still vividly recall every moment as if it occurred yesterday."

Even though I walk through the valley of the shadow of death, I will fear no evil, for you are with me; your rod and your staff, they comfort me. - Psalm 23:4

Chapter 21

To the Gap and Back?

Aimless Soul

"The Gap" is a peaceful and safe place. As the sun began to rise, I found myself sitting on the curb, contemplating my next steps. Fortunately, I was acquainted with some individuals in the vicinity, which provided a sense of comfort. The atmosphere was eerily quiet, almost resembling a ghost town. Suddenly, I heard the sound of an engine and saw a service truck pulling up to deliver goods to a nearby restaurant. I asked the driver if I could use his phone. To my relief, he agreed and even offered me a bottle of water, perhaps sensing my fatigue. With limited contacts memorized, I only recalled my brother David's phone number. I explained my situation to the driver, and he suggested contacting the sheriff. Following his advice, I placed a call to the sheriff's office.

I observed that people in Tennessee tended to be more compassionate compared to those in Kentucky. The sheriff who assisted me displayed genuine kindness and escorted me to the hospital in Harrogate for a thorough examination of my knee. However, I couldn't help but notice the shortcomings in the hospital's service. It seemed outdated and lacked efficiency. Despite this, the doctor administered a pain-relieving injection for my knee, and the social worker arranged transportation for me. Yet, the ride service was of little use since my ultimate destination was back home in Minnesota. The taxi driver returned me to the Middlesboro Holiday Inn, where this entire ordeal had unfolded.

I approached the hotel staff to retrieve information from my previous stay a few nights ago. I hoped this data might assist me in returning home or substantiating my innocence regarding the initial arrest. While there, I also requested access to the guest's computer to reach my Facebook page. Although it may appear trivial, it served as a means to alert those who knew me well that something was amiss, albeit without explicitly stating it. Instead, I posted nonsensical content, which is characteristic of manic writing.

The taxi driver had been waiting for me. However, when I requested to go to a different location, he stated he couldn't. Feeling helpless, I limped across the street to an AT&T store where I asked for assistance, even to use their phone. The employee on duty kindly gave me $7.

I was starving, so I decided to head to the nearby Cracker Barrel. With my limited funds, I ordered tea and a muffin. I was so famished. A family seated nearby overheard my discussion with the waitress about my financial struggles. Moved by my situation, they generously bought me a full meal and offered me a ride. Unsure of where to go, I suggested Lee County, Virginia, as I had friends there. It's not far from Middlesboro or Cumberland Gap. While we were on our way to Lee County, the father asked me if I knew the Lord Jesus.

I replied, *"Yes, I love Jesus. He's the reason I'm still alive."* The father asked again, *"Are you sure you know Jesus?"* I reassured him, *"Yes, I do. Thank you. I love him so much."*

The family dropped me off at the home where my old horse, Fancy, now lived. I had befriended this family back in April when I found out they had purchased Fancy from my old farrier. Mitch, the father of the girl who now owned. Fancy, was home.

He offered to call someone who could help me, though, looking back, I couldn't help but wonder why he couldn't assist himself. Soon, a couple of people arrived and brought me to a homeless shelter in Pineville, KY.

"Not Kentucky again," I thought. I'm sure Mitch was wondering why I was there and why I talked and acted the way I did.

Upon arriving at the Safe Haven Shelter, I found the people there very welcoming and supportive. Despite it being late, everyone was settling in for the night. However, try as I might, I couldn't seem to calm down. My mind raced, and I tossed and turned in bed. Eventually, I woke up one of the staff members and asked if he had any aspirin. Unfortunately, he became upset with me for waking him up and yelled at me to go back to bed. In my irritated and sleep-deprived state, I yelled back at him, not thinking straight. I then walked out of the shelter to get some fresh air. When I returned, I was informed that I was banned from the shelter and could never come back. This felt incredibly unfair, especially considering I had only been there briefly. Now, I wondered, *what should I do?*

Walking out of town along the highway, I felt a sense of directionlessness. Not far from town, a car pulled over, and a man and a woman offered me a ride. Gratefully, I accepted. During the ride, we chatted, and they shared that they worked at Arby's in Pineville but lived in Middlesboro. They also mentioned that they were Christians. They kindly drove me to Cumberland Gap, a place where I felt safe and comfortable.

In Cumberland Gap, I wandered aimlessly, my mind clouded with no clear destination in mind. People in the Gap are friendly and cherish its historical significance. Although my mind wasn't clear, I remember seeing Donnie, a Vietnam vet who lived in the Gap. I first met him in the spring of 2015 when I vacationed there. Donnie offered me food and a place to rest, providing a sense of safety and security like a father figure.

It must have been difficult for Donnie to see me in such a restless and irritable state. Mania can indeed cause behavior in ways that are not typical for me, leading to strained relationships and difficult situations. It's understandable to wish I hadn't experienced mania, but it's important to remember that it's a part of my journey and not a reflection of my character. Oh, I wished I had never been manic.

I wandered around the Cumberland Gap, my mind clouded with anxiety and paranoia. With the fear of the world ending and paranoia consistently running through my veins, I would hide out whenever I saw people in Cumberland Gap. Sometimes, I even believed the people I saw weren't human or were possessed by something otherworldly. It's astonishing how sleep deprivation and mania can distort perception. I'd find myself frozen in place in the park, fearing for my safety whenever someone came into view, regardless of their distance,

Reflecting on those moments, I shudder at the memories of my irrational behavior.

In that psychotic state of mind, I felt I needed to hide the beautiful ring I manically purchased weeks before my trip. The ring was a magnificent piece of jewelry adorned with a large topaz and diamonds that glittered in the light. The oval-shaped topaz sat elegantly in a polished white gold band, catching the light with every movement.

While I was thinking about the ring, I was already lying on the ground in the park downtown, hiding from any passersby. I sat up, looking around, making sure no one was near. I found a quiet spot under a couple of trees situated next to the benches. Carefully, I dug a small hole in the earth. Placing the ring inside, I covered it with dead leaves and soil. The trees sheltering the spot where I buried the ring stood on a raised bed, adding to the feeling of secrecy and seclusion.

To this day, I ponder whether that ring remains hidden in the hole I dug in Cumberland Gap. Only time will tell.
"Paranoia mixed with strong psychosis made for 'my precious' to be hidden for good."

He who dwells in the shelter of the Most High will abide in the shadow of the Almighty. I will say to the Lord, "My refuge and my fortress, my God, in whom I trust." Psalm 91:1-2

Chapter 22

Middlesboro to Pineville

Psychosis continues

Feeling a sense of security knowing my ring was hidden, I hastily fled towards the wooded area, consumed by panic. Maneuvering through the trees alongside the main road out of Cumberland Gap, I grappled with my fractured state of mind. Eventually, I reached the interstate highway outside the Gap and began trekking towards Virginia. It wasn't long before a sheriff spotted me and pulled up alongside me. It seemed law enforcement had become all too familiar with my plight.

Requesting to use a phone, I dialed my brother David's number, the only one I could recall. After a brief exchange between the sheriff and David, I finally got to speak with my brother, momentarily grounding me in reality. However, the connection was unstable, and I soon lost contact with them. In that fleeting moment, I feared it might be the last time I'd speak with family, convinced that impending calamity loomed.

The sheriff offered me a ride, bringing a glimmer of hope. Yet, to my dismay, he returned me to Middlesboro. Ahhhhhhhhh! Frustrated and bewildered, I couldn't comprehend why he failed to heed my brother's concerns. What I needed was medical attention, not a mere escort service shuttling me between states, landing me in either a jail cell or on a park bench.

No, there seemed to be a glaring lack of concern, as if they were just passing off this mentally ill individual from one place to another, from one state to the next. My recounting of events may not be perfectly chronological, but during this period, I was plunged into the deepest and most harrowing manic episode of my life. Ever. This psychotic state of thinking, mixed with no sleep and irrationality, was a train wreck.

Nestled in the heart of Kentucky lies Middlesboro, a colossal flat hole carved out by a meteorite. The sight of this geological wonder is both breathtaking and intriguing. Unsure why, but it had a magnetic pull on me, drawing me back time and time again. It's as if the dead pool of horror engulfed me here, and that's where I always ended up.

Stuck in Middlesboro for what felt like an eternity, I roamed its streets aimlessly, seeking refuge in shadows and finding solace in wooded sanctuaries. I distinctly remember traversing a bustling main street, accompanied by a kind-hearted man missing his left arm. In a gesture of compassion, he offered me his phone, allowing me to briefly reconnect with my brother, if only for a fleeting moment amidst the chaos.

"Please, David, please help me." I shared how my car was impounded in Middlesboro. I chatted away to him words that made sense to me, but to him, I'm sure, were utter nonsense.

Taking refuge from the blistering sun, I sought shade on a bench near the water fountain in downtown Middlesboro. I stayed by the fountain as long as I could to get out of the heat; I yearned for a drink of water.

I decided to continue on my way, hoping to find something or someone to help me. I made my way through the bustling town of Middlesboro on the main highway, and the scorching heat of midday began to take its toll on my body. Seeking solace from the oppressive temperature, I decided to take a break at the Middlesboro Mall. However, my hopes of finding relief were quickly dashed as I wandered through the corridors, feeling invisible amidst the throngs of shoppers. Disheartened, I emerged back into the sweltering heat, continuing my journey along the sun-drenched highway, oblivious to the fact that it led back to the town where I had been incarcerated, Pineville.

As dusk began to descend, I found myself at a mobile home sales business, where, in my state of delirium, I uttered nonsensical words. Sensing someone trailing me from the store, panic seized me, and I hastily sought refuge beneath one of the campers, suppressing my breath as the person's footsteps approached. They slowed down and began searching around as if they knew I was nearby. I didn't move an inch, fearing for my life After cautiously ensuring that the coast was clear, I silently slipped away and made my way towards a shadowy spot near the highway. With each step, I zigzagged across the road, darting from one parking lot to the next in a desperate attempt to evade detection. Eventually, I stumbled upon a doctor's office nestled into the hillside, its parking lot flanked by imposing rocks to forestall any potential mudslides.

Under the cover of darkness, I clambered up the side of the brick wall and surveyed the area, my heart pounding with trepidation. Spotting a police car nearby, I quickly nestled myself against the comforting bulk of a large rock, praying to remain unseen. Fear gnawed at my mind as I grappled with uncertainty, unsure of what fate awaited me. Exhaustion weighed heavily upon me, the relentless cycle of restlessness leaving me unsure when I had last found respite, sleep, or sustenance. Suddenly, the sound of footsteps crunching through the underbrush jolted me from my thoughts, sending a fresh wave of panic coursing through my veins.

A policeman said, *"Come on, let's go, Victoria."*

He didn't cuff me; he was kind. He just assisted me into the squad car.

The police ride was a quiet trip on the winding highway. It was a long, uneventful ride where I actually dozed off for a

moment. By now, the sun was starting to rise. The police brought me back to Pineville.

"Of all places!" I thought.

After they left me at the gazebo next to the Bell County Courthouse, I remained there for what felt like an eternity, paralyzed by fear and uncertainty. Every passing moment seemed fraught with peril, every shadow a potential threat. Yet, amid the chaos of my mind, one thing remained clear: the unwavering determination to cling to life.

Surveying my surroundings, I began to walk, my steps tentative and cautious. It was then that I noticed a statue of a German Shepherd, its proud form immortalized in bronze. Intrigued, I approached and read the plaque beneath, learning the story behind the statue. Memories of beloved pets from my past flooded my mind, and I found solace in the familiarity of their companionship.

Seeking respite from the oppressive heat, I settled onto a nearby bench, the cool metal offering a brief reprieve from the relentless sun. As sweat trickled down my brow, I closed my eyes, attempting to quiet the tumult of thoughts swirling within. Yet, try as I might, the specter of impending doom loomed large, casting a shadow over my attempts at tranquility.

It was then that an elderly man, his demeanor warm and genial, approached me. With a jovial belly and a gleaming bald head, he regaled me with tales of his family, his grandchildren, and the cherished memories of his own youth. In his presence, I felt a fleeting sense of familiarity, as though I were in the company of my own father once more. Nestled on my finger, the antique pearl ring glinted in the sunlight, a silent reminder of the ties that bind us to those we hold dear.

I thought it would be a nice gift for him, so I handed it to him and said, *"You have been so kind to me. Please use this as a gift."*

He smiled and became teary-eyed, saying, *"That's my daughter's birthstone."* The elderly man thanked me and went on his way. I sat there, soaking up the hot June sun.

I did stuff like this on a regular basis when I was severely manic. I would give things away randomly. Looking back, I hope it blessed this older man and his daughter. The Lord can take my crazy and turn it into good.

"I can only hope that through my mania, I was still able to bless others one way or another, even if it didn't make sense at the time."

Let your light shine before men in such a way that they may see your good deeds and moral excellence, and glorify your Father who is in heaven. Matthew 5:16

Chapter 23

Delirium

Refuge for my weary soul?

In Pineville, I often felt like an unwelcome intruder; my presence met with suspicion and uncertainty. Hours slipped away as I wandered the streets aimlessly, desperate for some semblance of refuge. One fateful night, as I found myself near the library, the sight of a police car approaching sent a surge of panic coursing through me. With trembling limbs, I pressed myself against the cool brick wall, praying to escape notice.

For agonizing moments, I stood frozen in place, my heart pounding in my chest. When I dared to open my eyes once more, the police car had vanished into the night, leaving behind only the echo of my racing pulse. Relief flooded through me like a balm, offering a brief respite from the relentless grip of fear.

Yet, even in the shadows, a beacon of light emerged in the form of a man clad in pristine white. His attire, a stark contrast to the darkness that enveloped us, seemed to illuminate the path ahead. With gentle reassurance, he reached out, his touch a lifeline in the tumult of uncertainty. Hand in hand, we traversed the sidewalk together, his presence a shield against the encroaching darkness. In his company, for the first time in what felt like an eternity, I found solace. No longer alone in the night, no longer haunted by the specter of fear, I walked with renewed purpose, guided by the unwavering support of a stranger turned savior.

We strolled together, exchanging stories and finding brief respite in shared laughter. Sensing my fatigue, the man suggested a moment of rest, leading me to a family's apartment where I could rejuvenate. I fell asleep in the tub for a while, and it felt great to rest. His friends offered me a sandwich and a soda and even gave me a change of clothes since mine were like filthy rags. Later on, the guy and I continued walking until we got to his friend's trailer home. It was quite dark as the house didn't have electricity. We spent some time there, chatting and socializing, although I mostly zoned out.

By morning, I was told by this friendly fellow that he had to go; he bid me farewell and left, walking up a hill nearby. I was delusional and confused. I embarked on a futile quest to trace his footsteps, stumbling through the sweltering heat in a haze of delusion and desperation. The heat by midday was scorching hot. I was so thirsty and loopy. I thought he could help me again; maybe he could help me get a hold of my family.

By now, I was so out of it I'm sure nothing I said made sense. I was hallucinating, completely irrational, just completely out of it. I honestly thought the world was ending. I walked by a woman jogging on the hill, and I thought she was half dead; she was so wrinkly. I came across another woman, whom I thought was my sister Rose, and she was dead, but walking on the street, and that's why I saw her. The boundaries between reality and illusion blurred beyond recognition, leaving me adrift in a nightmarish realm of my own creation. That's how delusional I was.

I just couldn't go on any further. I just couldn't. I stopped at a house with a porch and a nice picket fence. I climbed up the stairs to get out of the heat and rest. I fell asleep on the porch. I may have fallen asleep for a moment, minutes, an hour. Who really knows? I woke up spinning. I felt the world was upside down. A man was mowing his lawn next door. I just kept looking at him, thinking it was someone I knew.

I even said, *"Hi, Thomas!"* Poor guy must have thought, *"What a loony, who's on my neighbor's porch?"*

The owner of the home showed up along with a police officer. I wasn't handcuffed, but the police officer escorted me to the Pineville jail. When I was preparing for my booking photo, I noticed a hand-painted mural on the wall that displayed the Bell County Detention Center emblem. Being an artist myself, I became excited and started discussing the details of the mural with the officers in my manic state. They found my enthusiasm amusing, which is evident in my mug shot. After that ordeal, they led me down this nasty, gray, dingy hallway to a disgusting, cold cell. The cell was at the end of the hallway, nowhere near any other cell or entrance. All the paint was peeling off the walls, mold was growing on the ledges, and the shower had a brick ledge separating it from the floor. The shower drain was clogged with deep sludge and grimy water. The cell looked like something out of a horror movie. Actually, the whole jail did.

While I sat on the bench in this cell, I was so restless. No matter what I tried to do, I couldn't rest. I needed something to do, someone to talk to, something, anything. You see, when a manic person is put in a room with nothing to do or anyone to speak with, they will go more insane. Being manic, I need to be stimulated, need something to do, write, read, draw, talk with, anything. Of course, what I really needed was medication to bring me back to reality, but I didn't realize this; I was too out of it. Besides, I never recognized when I was manic.

The door to the cell was large, thick, and heavy, with a small slit near the bottom for the food tray. Dinner time rolled around, and my tray was placed in the slot for me to grab.

While the jailer placed the tray of food in the slot, I gently grabbed her hand, saying, *"Please help me."*

She yelled in her southern drawl, *"How dare you grab me!"*

She ran off down the hall and returned with another jailer with a God-forsaken metal chair. They came into the cell with the chair and forced me to sit in it. They strapped my legs to the chair using leg cuffs and strapped my left arm to the chair with another metal cuff, leaving my right arm to eat my meal. They left me in the chair for a while, coming back and asking if I wouldn't do that again and stay calm. I responded quietly with a *"yes, ma'am."* Afterward, I made such a mess of that already nasty cell. I took the water from the sink and "showered." My meals didn't end up in my stomach but instead in the swampy shower stall. I was angry with how I was treated, so I gave the already disgusting jail cell a bath.

I was released the next day, but low and behold, they couldn't find my clothes or shoes or my jewelry! Well, a jailer named Frannie found a huge pair of gray jogging pants and an oversized olive green t-shirt with the slogan "ugly ain't got no alibi" written in white on it. Oh my goodness, there I went, hobbling out the door midafternoon with oversized clothes, orange floppy jail sandals, and 'ugly ain't got no alibi.'

As I walked away from that old, filthy jail, the heat was already unbearable in the middle of the day. The humidity made it even more uncomfortable. Despite my knee pain, I strolled, my mind racing with thoughts of home, my childhood, and my parents.

While passing by the Pineville bank, I saw that the temperature was already 95 degrees at noon. Seeking relief from the heat, I stopped to sit in the gazebo near the Pineville courthouse. There, I saw two girls playing nearby, so I approached them and introduced myself. *"Hello! I'm Vicky,"* I said. *"What are your names?"*

The older girl bravely replied, *"I'm Sara, and this is my little sister, Ann. She's four, and I'm ten."* When I asked where they lived, Sara pointed to an old brick building across the street. She asked if I wanted to see it, and I agreed.

As we walked to the building, Sara proudly told me about the Davis Building's history. She said it was built in the 1800s and used to house many businesses and maybe even a theater. But as we climbed the stairs to their apartment, the building's peeling paint, dirty stairwell, and musty smell made me sad.

Their apartment was sparsely furnished and filthy, and the girls were dirty, too. Sara introduced me to her mother, Darla, a quiet woman, and her father, Eugene, who was also home. They offered me some Kool-Aid to drink, which I accepted. Sara then led me to their outdoor balcony, which was full of garbage and broken toys.

I offered to help clean up, but they seemed content with things as they were. Eugene shared that he had been unemployed for a while and needed help caring for his family. I mentioned I would help out as much as I could.

Sara's 13-year-old cousin Ginger came to visit and invited Sara to go to the city pool, but Sara declined. I offered to go instead and walked with Ginger to the pool, talking her ear off along the way. After a seven-block walk, we arrived at the fenced-in pool area. I was excited to swim, but I didn't have a swimsuit. I found some red shorts with black polka dots in the girls' changing room, put them on with my black sports bra, and left my jogging pants and olive green 'ain't got no alibi' t-shirt on a bench. I dove into the deep end and swam as far as I could. The sensation of swimming underwater made me feel alive and free. I swam as far as I could and then floated on the water, gazing up at the beautiful blue sky. When the pool closed, and it started to get dark, I grabbed my clothes and walked until I found a car lot. I changed back into my pants and threw the shorts away in an alley garbage bin. I kept walking through the town until I reached the highway that looped through Pineville, 25E.

I am uncertain how long I was in Pineville, but I know I kept trying to leave. My mind wouldn't turn off; my body controlled by my crazy mind-tangled in a mess of short circuits of words and thoughts that would never stop. I can only imagine what I looked like. I'm sure my face was marked in delirium, with my hair raggedly tangled. My cheeks sunken in from lack of eating. Oversized clothes that were dirty from lying on the ground hung on my body. My eyes were wild and crazy from mania streaming through my veins. I was a mess. Period.

My mug shot haunted me for a long time. Anyone could find it on search engines because someone took my mug shot and shared it. A relative informed me that it was easy to find by typing my name on the internet. When I searched for it back in 2016, I was beyond humiliated when I found it. I thought about sharing it in this book, but unfortunately, the mug shot is gone. I have tried everything to find it, but the Bell County Detention Center informed me when I recently contacted them, that the records from that time were lost due to their computer system shutting down.

I can easily access my records through the Kentucky judicial court system, but unfortunately, I cannot retrieve my mug shot. The picture was very distressing for me and brought back memories of

Difficult time. I was manic, sleep-deprived, and talked non-stop. Additionally, I looked utterly disabled in the picture, and I believe that the jailer who took the photo deliberately made me look that way. I was admiring the hand-painted mural of Bell County's Jail emblem and complimented the artist who created it, saying,

"Wow, whoever did this is a great artist! I'm an artist, too!" I was looking up at the mural as the camera captured the moment. I hope that people learn to treat others with kindness and respect, especially during difficult times when we all need love and support.

"I've always wondered what it would be like to see myself from another's point of view. I can only imagine what people thought of me."

Resist him, firm in your faith, knowing that the same kinds of suffering are being experienced by your brotherhood throughout the world. 1 Peter 5:9

Chapter 24

Truly Homeless

Living Nightmare

Being in Pineville felt like riding a spine-chilling roller coaster with no end in sight. Every step I took, every turn I made, seemed to prolong the terrifying journey, engulfing me in fear and uncertainty. Whether I was trudging along the highway, feeling the blistering heat on my skin, or meandering through the streets of Pineville, desperately seeking genuine help, the sensation of being ensnared never waned.

Every encounter with another person became an opportunity to plead for assistance, to borrow a phone and reach out to my siblings for rescue. Yet, in my distress, I struggled to articulate my needs clearly. Nonetheless, my family did their best to come to my aid.

I felt utterly powerless, unable to break free from the harsh reality that had engulfed my life. Each day was a relentless battle to come to terms with my circumstances, the burden of which weighed heavily upon me. It was as though I was trapped in a never-ending nightmare, unable to rouse myself from its grip.

Fear gripped my every move, lost and alone in a foreign land, or should I say foreign to a Northerner like me. There I was in complete bewilderment about what was going on or why I was on this road; I was just being me, or so I thought. I don't even recall exactly where I was that night; I know I was so frightened. (I recently looked at a map and found I was on Wilderness Road Heritage Highway)

This night, like so many I've had in this living nightmare, was too close to death. I was walking for hours in the middle of the night down a winding highway—hours that turned into days and weeks.

After hours of walking in the dark, not having a clue of the time or where I was, and not knowing anyone, I needed a break. Thirst clawed at my throat, hunger gnawed at my stomach, and exhaustion weighed heavily on my weary frame. My parched throat burned with each labored breath, and my head throbbed with the relentless ache of dehydration, exacerbated by the sweltering summer heat. I felt I couldn't move anymore; my bones ached—my soul broken, my body desperate. With a heavy heart, I paused, seeking respite from the relentless march of despair. Collapsing to the ground, I felt the dampness of the humid air seep into the grass beneath me. Laying there in the dark, feeling the dew, I gingerly tried to suck some of it from the grass. I was so parched from walking for days.

Determined, I gained strength to keep going, yet as I walked in the blackness of midnight, I got entangled in some large weeds and vines, causing me to tumble downhill toward a river next to the highway. It's pitch black, I'm alone and so scared, I thought I would end up in the river entwined in the weeds and never found it. Those thoughts ran through my mind as I wrestled my way back to solid ground.

Eventually, I stumbled upon a spot along the road where light filtered through the branches of the oak and maple trees, crowning the bluffs. With a glimmer of hope igniting within me, I began ascending the winding driveway, clinging to the chance of encountering someone who could offer assistance.

There it was, *a haven place,* I thought to myself, *"Maybe here I could find rest and a drink."*

I knocked and knocked, and finally, an elderly lady answered the door.

But she barely cracked it open, saying, *"Go away, it's late!"* She seemed frightened by my presence and shut the door.

Who knows what time it was? I hadn't a clue. I stayed in her yard, hoping that maybe in the daylight, she would help me, but instead, I heard a car slowly climbing the steep driveway. I hid behind a tree slouched on a steep hill, and sure enough, it was the police. I didn't move or make a sound; I sat motionless behind that tree. I'd had enough horrifying experiences with law enforcement in the past. The police officer shone his spotlight through the yard and trees. I could hear my heart pounding in my chest. I held my breath, closed my eyes, and prayed the police would leave. Moments later, he was gone. I still sat there motionless just in case… just in case he would return and do what others had done before.

With the police officer gone, I didn't opt for the winding driveway. Instead, I plunged into the dense trees, each step quickening the beat of my heart. The steep descent felt endless, but I was resolute in my determination to reach the highway below. Relying on the sturdy trees and dense shrubbery, I descended the perilous slope, my hands clutching onto their rough bark for stability as I cautiously made my way down. The fear of a potential fall lingered, haunting me with the thought of being discovered by either the police officer or the resident of the nearby home.

Once I reached the highway, I walked and walked. My feet hurt, I was so tired, I just needed rest. I came to a house along the highway. I looked around and didn't see anyone. I peered in the windows, and it appeared no one was home, or I hoped no one was. I was afraid of a repeat of the previous house. There was an unlocked shed near the house, so I crawled inside to rest and fell asleep briefly because I didn't want to get caught. That night was cold compared to previous nights; I did what I could to stay warm by curling up in a ball. I even covered myself with a piece of cardboard.

I headed on my way, walking on that lonely highway. I eventually reached a gas station. By now, the dawn was barely lighting the tree line. I was so relieved to see someone was there. I asked for a drink or any kind of help. He just shrugged his shoulders and said, *"You can try the bathroom."*

So, I did. I drank from the faucet in the bathroom and continued on my way. Where? I didn't know; I just kept walking.

The sun was peering over the trees while I walked along the highway when a car pulled over. It was a man and a woman around my age. They asked if I would like a lift to town.

"Thank God!" I thought.

I nodded in appreciation and expressed my gratitude to them. As we talked, they mentioned their move from Michigan to Middlesboro and their faith as Christians. Their kindness in offering me a bottle of water was deeply appreciated. They dropped me off at the Middlesboro Mall, bringing me back once again to familiar surroundings in Middlesboro.

As I wandered around Middlesboro, I made my way to the nursing home I used to work at to rest my weary legs. It wasn't long before a sheriff showed up.

This time, the officer asked, *"Is there anyone you can go see or somewhere you can go?"*

I mentioned my dad's old Appalachian buddy in Lee County, Virginia, not far from Middlesboro. He offered to take me there. I was relieved, thinking I would be seeing a familiar face, my dad's good buddy. We arrived at the Appalachian man's house, driving up his long driveway. The sheriff assisted me out of the vehicle; the Appalachian man was outside.

He shouted, *"Get her the fuck off my property!!"*

I couldn't believe it. Why? He knew me my entire life, and now this? I was devastated. I thought he would help me get home.

The sheriff brought me back to Pineville. I cried most of the drive to Pineville. He assisted me out of his vehicle and said, *"Is there someone you can call?"* I said, *"Yes, my brother David."* He dialed the number and handed me the phone. My sister-in-law Kim answered the phone. I asked her for help. The call ended, and the sheriff left me there, so I walked to the gazebo next to the courthouse and sat and cried

"I truly felt like I was in a nightmare, and people were out to get me. Delirious from so many nights without sleep caused such severe psychosis."

Turn to me and be gracious to me, for I am lonely and afflicted. The troubles of my heart are enlarged; bring me out of my distresses. Psalm 25:16-17

Chapter 25

Let's go for a ride

Freedom!

While sitting in the gazebo, drained and defeated, I noticed a gathering of people down the street. They seemed jovial and engaged, some of them youthful. Intrigued, I decided to investigate and found them entering an old building, so I followed along. While in the restroom, I stumbled upon a pair of lady's jeans beneath the sink cabinet, so I swapped them for my own and stashed my old pants in a bag.

As the church service concluded and attendees began to disperse, I found myself outside, utterly fatigued. Leaning against the wall, tears welled up in my eyes. It was then that the youth pastor approached me, inquiring if I was alright or in need of assistance. Relief washed over me, anticipating that he would offer aid in getting me home or perhaps contacting my family. However, to my dismay, he opted to summon the police instead.

I wept and wept, thinking, *'Not again!'* A police officer showed up and spoke with the youth pastor.

I couldn't hear what they were saying; I just continued to cry hysterically. The police officer got on the phone. Next thing, he walked up to me and stated, *"Your brother contacted me and paid for your car to get out of impound."*

The police officer kindly escorted me to Joe's Towing, where my car awaited. Freedom at last! Despite still lacking money or a phone, the overwhelming sense of liberation washed over me. However, as I entered my Chevy, I was greeted by an unpleasant odor of rotting fish. Joe, the owner of the tow yard, pointed out the source: a pair of pants on the back seat containing the decaying fish. Reflecting on the absurdity of the situation, I couldn't help but wonder what Sam and I had been thinking.

Nevertheless, with my Chevy back in my possession, I decided to return to my sanctuary, Cumberland Gap. I had some artwork for sale at the Frame Shop, which I had brought with me during my vacation in April 2015. One of my pieces had sold for $80, providing me with some much-needed funds. With this newfound financial resource, I pondered how best to utilize it. Only time would tell.

I stopped at Donnie's, the Vietnam vet, to say hello, and he invited me to stay again. Now, one huge problem, my car and all my belongings smelled horrendous. Fish. Rotten, stinky, hot, slimy fish. That fish Sam caught rotted for who knows how long in my car. Well, I didn't think twice; I didn't care because I had my stuff! I stayed at Donnie's, cleaned up, and slept well that night. It would have been my first natural sleep in a very long time. It wasn't a whole night, but at least it felt good to rest. The following day,

Cumberland Gap was bustling with the excitement of the White Lightning festival. Thinking of my friend Martha and her family back in Pineville, I couldn't resist the urge to share in the festivities with them. Hastily, I made my way back to Donnie's place to retrieve my belongings, feeling a rush of joy at having them back in my possession. The sweltering heat outside prompted me to change into a swimsuit and a long tank top, a peculiar choice given the lack of any nearby swimming spots. It was just how my mind worked in those manic moments, devoid of logical reasoning.

Eager to treat Martha's family to a memorable experience, I embarked on the 15-mile journey to Pineville and extended an invitation to Martha and her youngest daughter to join me at Cumberland Gap. To my surprise, they had never visited the Gap before, hindered by transportation limitations and financial constraints. Additionally, Martha's friend, in need of a ride to Middlesboro, accompanied us on the trip.

Before immersing ourselves in the festivities of White Lightning, I wanted to share the breathtaking view from the Pinnacle overlook with my guests. However, our ascent up the winding hill came to an abrupt halt when my car sputtered to a stop just shy of reaching the summit - I had neglected to monitor the gas gauge, a consequence of my manic state.

Overlook

After my car stalled on the way up the hill, leaving Martha and her companions waiting in the car, I resolved to seek assistance from passersby. Descending the winding road in my conspicuous attire - a long tank top and swimsuit - I caught the attention of a well-to-do family from Illinois traveling in a luxurious Cadillac. They graciously offered me a ride to Walmart, where they not only purchased a gas can for me but also filled it up.

Grateful for their kindness, I accompanied them back to the base of the park overlook, where they dropped me off. Laden with the heavy jug of gas, I began the arduous trek back up the hill to where my Chevy had stalled. However, to my dismay, as I neared the top, I watched as my Chevy rumbled past me, with Martha at the wheel!

Oh man, *"Wait!!"* I yelled.

I waved down a red '95 truck heading down the hill to stop. A friendly local man driving, a little on the chunky side, gave me a ride.

I said, *"Catch up with that Chevy!"*

He said, *"I'll try, but got I this old truck here!"* I watched as she drove away, down the highway towards Pineville. Oh man, please, please don't go too far. Thankfully, she pulled over in one of my OTHER favorite places, Holiday Inn! I got out and said to Martha, *"Why did you do that!?"*

She explained that her friend offered to turn the vehicle around and try to coast. As they did that, the police showed up and arrested him. Not sure why - Drugs? Martha's poor little daughter Emily was so afraid of all the commotion from the police that she wet herself in the backseat. Poor thing. I gave her a small long shirt I had so she could be dry.

We never made it to the overlook. Imagine that.

Off we went to the Gap for the festival. I wanted to treat them. The Gap has an artist's co-op; that's where I made the $80. So I took that money and paid for Emily's games and pizza. Martha and Emily were tired, and they were both ready to go home. Prior to us leaving, I asked them to hold on to some of my belongings at their home to make room for them in the backseat.

When we got back to their home, Sara said, *"Thank you for the computer."* I just looked at her strangely, not knowing what she meant. It wasn't until months later I realized that they had stolen my computer.

"To this day, I laugh, visualizing myself running after my Chevy in a tank top and swim suit. That day was incredible insane!"

He will yet fill your mouth with laughter, and your lips with shooting. Job 8:21

Chapter 26

Beyond Complete Psychosis

This was it; 3rd time.

I was still feeling wide awake and eager for some excitement, so I decided to return to Cumberland Gap. As I arrived, I made a stop at a small, rundown bar that had once been a laid-back spot but had now transformed into a popular hangout for college students. I had met the manager months earlier, and he had been friendly back then, but this time, his attitude toward me had changed.

As I chatted with people outside the bar, and he with his macho attitude, long hair, and big biceps, said, *"Get out of here!"* I said, *"No, I don't have to; I'm not in your bar."*

He continued to yell and tell me to get off the property. At one point, he got on his knees, stuck his cheek out toward me, and said, *"Hit me."* I said, *"Why would I do that?"*

I got into my car and drove back into Middlesboro; it was already around 11:30 pm. I found myself once again at the familiar Holiday Inn. Upon entering, I struck up conversations with some younger individuals who had been on a mission trip and were passing through. Engaging them in conversation, I eagerly wanted to share photos, so I fetched my expensive camera. However, as I began showing them pictures, they excused themselves and headed to their rooms. Undeterred, I made my way to the guest computer, intending to connect with people through Facebook. Before long, two police officers entered the lobby and placed me under arrest. My camera remained abandoned on the table as they escorted me first to the local jail in Middlesboro for booking and then to Bell County. This marked my third arrest.

It was well into the night when they placed me in a cell situated near the jail's main entrance. Surprisingly, this cell was relatively clean compared to others I had been in. It lacked a shower, offering only a toilet and a raised cement platform resembling a bed, about six inches off the ground. An old, thin green *"mattress"* and a small, gray wool-like blanket were provided for sleeping, but there was no pillow. Despite my exhaustion, sleep eluded me. The cell lacked a slot for meal trays, and I tossed and turned on the uncomfortable green mat, still buzzing from the events in Cumberland Gap.

The next day, a staff member brought me my breakfast tray. I finished the meal quickly and then found myself at a loss for things to do. To distract myself from the anxiety and monotony of my surroundings, I began to sing. I sang whatever songs popped into my head, finding some solace and relief in the act of singing, and I also noticed I could hear a guy or two say, *"Keep singing."* if I stopped. I got on my tippy toes and saw there was a cell kiddy corner from mine with guys in it. After being served a lackluster dinner of a bland hotdog on a soggy bun, accompanied by limp fries and a plastic cup that required filling from the faucet connected to the toilet, I found myself asking what day it was. To my surprise, it was Saturday. Attempting to pass the time and alleviate my restlessness, I began to sing to myself. However, my efforts were quickly thwarted by Mean Jean, the jailer on duty, who rudely demanded that I cease singing. Despite her interruption, I couldn't resist the urge to continue singing softly, finding solace in the simple act amidst the monotony of the jail cell.

When the compassionate jailer came to collect my tray, I mustered the courage to ask her for a pen and paper. Desperate to quiet the chaos swirling in my mind, I felt an overwhelming urge to write. She kindly provided me with a pen tube and a piece of paper, and without hesitation, I began to pour my thoughts onto the page. Scribbling down random musings, fragments of poetry, or whatever else came to mind, I found solace in the act of putting pen to paper, if only for a fleeting moment.

While I wrote, I sang. Mean Jean came back this time saying, *"You stop now; you gonna go in the chair."*

Sure enough, Mean Jean, accompanied by her sidekick, brought the chair, and I was firmly strapped into it. They handled me roughly, coercing me into the chair and securing each restraint with a relentless grip. My waist, shoulders, wrists, and ankles were all bound tightly, rendering me completely immobile. I couldn't so much as budge. Fueled by nervous energy, I found myself instinctively wiggling my feet, the only part of me that retained any semblance of movement. The chains jingled softly with each hesitant movement as I sat there, quietly singing to myself. The familiar strains of a worship song, *"Come Now Is the Time to Worship,"* filled the air, providing a fleeting sense of solace amidst the chaos.

Mean Jean returned minutes later, issuing a stern warning that I needed to cease all noise and movement, threatening to douse me with pepper spray if I didn't comply. (If only she had received better training in dealing with individuals with mental illness.) Despite her request, I found myself unable to stop. I continued to sing softly to myself, whispering the lyrics and nervously wiggling my feet. When Mean Jean returned with the pepper spray poised and ready, accompanied by two other jailers, fear and helplessness washed over me. Tears welled up in my eyes as I contemplated the imminent threat. I promised to stop, pleading with them to listen, and thankfully, they relented, leaving me in the chair. I took deep breaths, humming ever so softly, determined not to provoke them further. With each breath in and out, tears streamed down my face as I longed for the comfort of home, my heart pounding in my chest with a mixture of fear and anguish.

As time crawled by, I lost all sense of its passage. Was it night or day? Minutes felt like hours, and hours like days. The pressing need to relieve myself grew unbearable, but I hesitated to call out for help, fearing Mean Jean's wrath and the sting of pepper spray. Desperation overwhelmed me, and tears of frustration streamed down my cheeks as I struggled to maintain control. In the end, I couldn't hold it any longer. The humiliation of wetting myself in that cold, metal chair was a bitter blow to my already fragile dignity. Whether they noticed on the surveillance cameras or simply coincidentally, two jailers returned and released me from the chair. I confessed what had happened, and they provided me with clean pants, a small reprieve from the shame of my accident. With no shower available, I changed into the fresh orange jumpsuit, the only article of clothing that truly belonged to me being my old black sports bra.

Later that day, Mean Jean barged into my cell to check on me, her presence like a dark cloud looming over me. Disgusted by her treatment of me, I couldn't resist making a snide remark under my breath. When she demanded to know what I said, I responded with a defiant act of rebellion, giving her a glimpse of my rear end. It was a small gesture, but it provoked a loud and angry response from her. She threatened consequences, but thankfully, she refrained from strapping me into the chair again. Instead, she slapped me with a charge of indecent exposure in jail, adding insult to injury in an already humiliating situation.

Not able to rest, I would do whatever I could to entertain myself. Thankfully, I had the makeshift pen (the tube of ink with the tip), the one the jailer gave me. I could still write some. I already wrote a ton on the one piece of paper I had, so I started writing on the walls. I wrote the National Anthem, drew the flag, wrote my name and other folks' names, and wrote the different jailers and who was good and who was terrible. Surprisingly, no jailer showed up to stop me.

The next day, the head jailer, Steve, made an unexpected appearance at my cell. After a cursory glance, he exchanged a few words with his colleagues before departing. Later, the compassionate jailer, Heidi, informed me that Steve had ordered an evaluation for me. It wasn't until much later that I learned my sister, Roseann, had tirelessly advocated for me, urging authorities in Bell County to recognize that I needed medical attention, not confinement. At the time, though, I remained oblivious to the gravity of my situation or the necessity for intervention.

Subsequently, two sheriffs escorted me on a journey through the winding hills and mountains of Southern Kentucky to Harlan, where I was admitted to the psychiatric unit for evaluation.

"Feisty, crazy lady, singing her lungs out and driving the jailers mad - me."

The tongue also is a fire, a world of evil among the parts of the body. It corrupts the whole body, sets the whole course of one's life on fire, and is itself set on fire by hell. James 3:6

Chapter 27

Let's take a look

Evaluation - hospital

In this mental health ward, I encountered a diverse array of individuals, each with their own unique quirks and qualities - but then again, that's to be expected in such a setting. One individual who left a lasting impression on me was Katy. With her cherubic features and fiery red hair, she exuded a warmth that was hard to ignore. She looked at me, saying, *"You got nothing but orange on!"*

"How about I give you a shirt? I got tons of clothes here." The shirt I wore was a long T-shirt with stripes, a rather stylish choice. During our time in the psych unit, Katy opened up about her own story, revealing that she had been driven to a fit of rage by mistreatment from someone and ended up taking their life.

"Well, ya never know," I thought.

She had a variety of personal items with her, including shoes, clothes, and even books.

I slyly said, *"Look how cool these orange flip-flops I have; aren't they the best! These orange flip-flops are fun to wear and perfect for the pool."*

She grinned with her missing tooth shining through her smile and freckles gleaming. She said, *"Have these, I'll trade you!* Those flip-flops were adorable, blue with delicate flowers adorning them, and they've stayed with me ever since. Another individual, Steve, greeted me shyly as he passed by. He was a good kid, homeless, and not from around here like me. Despite his eccentricities, he was intelligent and kind-hearted. Steve generously offered me a pair of black gym shorts, allowing me to rid myself of the orange attire finally.

As I lay in bed, I found solace in the simple comforts surrounding me: a warm shower, a soft bed, and the compassionate faces of those nearby. The sensation of hot water cascading over me in the shower became a sanctuary, a temporary escape from the turmoil and uncertainty that engulfed me. Seated on the shower floor, I allowed the rhythmic flow of water to soothe away the tension in my body, feeling a sense of tranquility wash over me. Lost in the embrace of the moment, I drifted into sleep.

Upon awakening, I realized I had spent an extended period in the shower, and the nurse was now knocking on the door, expressing concern for my well-being. Assuring her I was nearly finished, I remained in the shower a while longer, relishing the warmth and comfort it provided, a brief respite from the challenges I faced.

Despite my initial resistance, Nurse Mary persisted in her care for me, even in the face of my harsh words and unkind remarks. I remember how her voice grated on my nerves, its sharpness piercing through my frustration. In moments of anger, lashed out, calling her names and casting hurtful words her way. Yet, through it all, she remained steadfast, offering me a level of care and compassion that I didn't feel deserving of.

Looking back, I see now how she acted as a mother figure to me, nurturing and guiding me through my struggles, even when I pushed her away. Her unwavering dedication to my well-being, despite my abrasive behavior, stands as a testament to her kindness and commitment to her role as a caregiver.

Pace, pace, sleep

One particular night stands out in my memory, a night when I drove the night staff to the brink of their patience. Restlessness consumed me, and I found myself pacing the floors relentlessly, flouting the rules by flicking on lights in the hallway and engaging the staff in conversation. My energy was boundless, my voice loud and echoing through the corridors, likely disrupting the sleep of my fellow residents.

The following day, I reached a breaking point after enduring weeks upon weeks of sleep deprivation and intense manic psychosis, a state of mind where I remained blissfully unaware of my own condition. Once again consumed by agitation, I resumed my pacing in the hallway, heedless of the disturbance it caused to those around me.

I was loud, yelling things like, *"I've been rapped."* Not long after, a few nurses arrived, restraining me and administering a shot, the elusive magic shot that swiftly ushered me into tranquility. Whether it was Haloperidol, Lorazepam, or a combination of both, I couldn't discern. Drifting off to sleep in my room, I surrendered to the embrace of slumber, its duration a mystery to me. It felt as though days passed before I stirred awake.

Upon waking, a sense of calm enveloped me, replacing the tumultuous torrent of thoughts that had plagued me before. I found myself conversing with Nurse Mary, expressing remorse for my earlier behavior. To my surprise, she was understanding and compassionate. In a gesture of kindness, she gifted me a cozy pair of socks and a pack of peanut M&Ms, a small but comforting token that spoke volumes amidst the chaos of my mind.

She whispered, *"Hide these so no one steals them."* She must have pitied me some.

The doctor who saw me on a regular basis was very odd, interesting, but definitely odd. He had a strong Indian accent and spoke in a way that made me wonder. He would start a sentence, pause for a while, stare off, then finish what he had to say. I was stuck in his office once when another resident acted out, and all the doors had to be shut and locked to protect everyone else; after examining me while in the hospital, he prescribed Lithium and Paxil. Lithium has been a stable drug for me since I was first diagnosed with bipolar type 1. Paxil, on the other hand, I wasn't sure how it would affect me. Now that my mind was clear, I found myself able to piece together the events of the past weeks with greater clarity. I remember being arrested on July 26th, admitted to the hospital on July 29th, and now it was July 5th. It was during this time that my brother Greg reached out to me while I was still in the hospital. His call brought me a sense of comfort and relief, a pleasant surprise amidst the chaos.

Although, in my frustrations of being in a hospital, I said to him, *"Greg, get me the FUCK out of here."* That's not a typical way for me to talk.

"Ativan, the medication that worked. I may have been horrible to others in the hospital, patient and staff alike, but the true me would have been helping not cursing them out."

Let no corrupting talk come out of your mouths, but only such as is good for building up, as fits the occasion, that it may give grace to those who hear. Ephesians 4:29

Facility:

Harlan ARH

Patient Name:

ROSC, VICTORIA

Date of Birth:
04/12/1977

EXAMINATION

LEGAL STATUS AT TIME OF ADMISSION

The patient was brought in under a 202A by the Bell County Detention Center.

CHIEF COMPLAINT

"I have nothing wrong with me. I am here because the police do not like me."

HISTORY OF PRESENT ILLNESS

This is a 38-year-old Caucasian female admitted to the services of ██████ The patient presented to the emergency room, brought by the Bell County Detention Center, for psychiatric evaluation. Petitioner was ██████████ from the Bell County Detention Center. The patient was evaluated by a qualified mental health professional, who listed that the patient was brought to them under a 202A from jail. The petitioner stated the patient is out of touch with reality, hallucinating. She was sleeping on a stranger's porch when they picked her up. She has been violent with their staff, removed her clothing, says she is not sleeping and has a history of bipolar. The patient is not on medications. The patient stated that she has possible PTSD. She is a mental health worker in Minnesota. The patient has not been on medications since September of 2014. According to qualified mental health professional, the patient needs further evaluation as she poses a risk of harm for self as well as jail staff. The goal is to evaluate, stabilize and return to jail. According to the petition, the 202A, the patient had been lodged in the Bell County Detention Center after being from Holiday Inn in Middlesboro, Kentucky. She was sleeping on the front porch, also located on an individual's porch sleeping. She was charged with 2 counts of criminal trespass, 3rd degree, disorderly conduct, and indecent exposure in jail. The patient reported to the police that someone had stolen her medicines and that is why she had not been taking them.

The patient noted to have "doodled" on her ankles and legs and back where she could reach because she became bored in jail. She does not have any tattoos. The patient's thoughts are racing and delusional. The patient denied having suicidal thoughts or ever having suicidal thoughts. The patient has flight of ideas during our conversation, distractibility, grandiosity, activity increase, talkativeness. She appears to be anxious, is fidgety during this interview in her seat. The patient's thoughts are very scattered. She jumps from subject to subject

PAST PSYCHIATRIC HISTORY

The patient states that she was hospitalized in Minnesota for manic behavior relating to bipolar. She does not have a psychiatrist or therapist that she sees. She denies attempting suicide or having self-mutilative behavior. She denies any chemical abuse history. She does not smoke or use illicit drugs.

253

PAST MEDICAL AND SURGICAL HISTORY

1. Patient reports that in November 2014, she possibly had a heart attack

2. She reports having seasonal allergies.

3. She reports a stress echo performed in December 2014.

4. Gallbladder removed in 2012.

5. ACL repair in 2003.

CURRENT MEDICATIONS

The patient was ordered Paxil 10 mg p.o. daily on admission, which she has refused to take, as she sees no need of it.

ALLERGIES

PATIENT DENIES ANY ALLERGIES TO FOOD OR DRUGS BUT REPORTS HAVING A SENSITIVITY FOR SIDE EFFECTS OF DRUGS.

Education: The patient states she graduated from high school and has 3 years of college but no degree. She does have a driver's license. Her hobbies include being an artist, a musician, writes poetry, is currently filming a movie. She is a mental health specialist

Spiritual religious preference is nondenominational, Christianity.

MENTAL STATUS EXAM

The patient is dressed appropriate for stated age and weather. Interaction is cooperative. The patient almost takes over the interview as she jumps from topic to topic and has to be brought back to the subject at hand. Speech pressured. Mood elated, euphoric. Affect blunted. She denies any suicidal or homicidal ideation. She denies auditory or visual hallucinations. She does express or display delusional behavior. It is confirmed that patient has achieved some of the things that she has told staff, such as she has worked in mental facilities before. She has went to college. She does sing for pleasure. However, she has built up on these talents to the extent that they are grandiose. She believes she is writing a book. She believes that she is a poet. She is slightly paranoid, as she is suspicious of those around her. She is unsure of why she is here. She thinks people from the jail, people from Middlesboro do not like her, and that is why they have sent her here. She is alert and oriented x3. Memory and cognition are adequate. Judgment and insight are limited. Thought process, flight of ideas, tangentiality. The patient also rambles.

APPALACHIAN REGIONAL HEALTHCARE, INC.

Harlan ARH Hospital

81 Ball Park Road

Harlan, KY 40831

Authenticated by ████████, MD On 07/05/2015 08:32:07 PM

Chapter 28

Jail Time

Freedom?

On July 6th, the doctor said I was better, and he would discharge me. I was elated; I thought, *"This is it; I am going back home to Minnesota!"* No, instead, two sheriffs show up, shackle my hands and ankles, and escort me back to Bell County Jail.

As I sat in the squad car, gazing out the window, a heavy blanket of depression descended upon me, constricting my chest and stealing my breath. Thoughts of being stranded in this unfamiliar terrain, far from the comfort of home and the embrace of loved ones, clouded my mind. I yearned for the familiar sights and sounds of Minnesota, but they felt distant, almost unreachable. The palpable sense of loneliness weighed heavily on me, threatening to overwhelm me with its suffocating embrace. Fear gnawed at the edges of my consciousness, leaving me wondering if I would ever find my way back to the sanctuary of home.

Upon returning to the jail, I was relegated to a solitary cell. Sleep became my only refuge; I lacked the appetite to eat, consumed as I was by distress. The following day, I was summoned to what they called court, although it felt nothing like the conventional notion of a courtroom. Instead, I stood before a camera, unable to see the judge but hearing his voice as he levied charges against me: disorderly conduct and trespassing, twice over. He set a bond of $1000, a stark reminder of the precariousness of my situation.

As I stood there, a woman with scraggly blonde hair and blue eyes approached and greeted me with a calm *"Hey you, how ya doing?"*

I was uncertain how to navigate the dynamics of the jail cell, surrounded by unfamiliar faces and confined within its cramped confines. Sensing my unease, a woman named Amber extended a gesture of kindness, inviting me to place my mat beside hers. Grateful for the offer of companionship, I accepted and settled down on the hard floor next to her. Amber's friendly demeanor prompted her to strike up a conversation, inquiring about my background and the circumstances that led me to our shared confinement. Reluctantly, I shared snippets of information about myself, feeling a sense of isolation amidst the group.

In the dimly lit cell, I counted a total of twelve other women, making me the thirteenth occupant in our crowded space. I noticed a small cracked TV in the corner of the floor. I dare not ask or even request a show, I didn't know what to expect from these women. Amber's offer to accommodate me near her provided a small sense of comfort amidst the unfamiliar surroundings, offering me a solitary connection in an otherwise alien environment.

A jailer came to our door, stating it was dinner time. I was kind of happy since I did feel a little hungry and thought we would be going out to a dining area. Nope. We lined up while we were able to walk one by one to a tray holder and grab a tray, bring it back to our repulsive cell to eat. With one table, we sure weren't all gonna fit, so we did what we could. Eat on the floor. The food was always gross, minimal, and very bland. This time around, a hamburger, baked beans, a mini powdered drink mix, and a small plastic cup for water from the toilet faucet. *How delicious!* Rolling my eyes. Unlike some of the other women who received care packages from friends and family, I had nothing to call my own. Amber's gesture of offering me an empty pop bottle of water and a powdered drink mix provided a small semblance of normalcy in an otherwise bleak situation.

Bunked on the opposite side of Amber was Suzie, a young woman with fiery auburn hair styled in a pixie cut. From the moment she arrived, Suzie made her presence known with her boisterous chatter and tendency to overshare. She regaled us with tales of her affluent family, her adoring boyfriend, and her impending transfer to a prison in Northern Kentucky. Suzie didn't shy away from revealing the dark details of her past, proudly recounting her alleged involvement in the death of her ex-boyfriend through stabbing.

Despite her shocking revelations, Suzie appeared almost innocuous in her demeanor, more like a spoiled, attention-seeking girl from Southern Kentucky than someone capable of such a heinous act. However, the veracity of her claims remained uncertain, leaving us to ponder whether she lived in a twisted fantasy world or if there was truth to her unsettling confessions. Regardless, Suzie's time among us was short-lived, as she was eventually whisked away to face the consequences of her actions, leaving behind a cloud of uncertainty and speculation in her wake.

Cellmate

With a woman leaving and no one else eager to claim the lower bunk in our cramped cell, I found myself both relieved and apprehensive about having a bit more space and privacy. The cell, originally intended for four occupants, now housed twelve of us. The two "bedrooms" within the cell had doors that could be shut by the jailers, a feature I would soon come to understand the significance of.

Among my cellmates was Julie, a stout, dark-haired woman with hair cascading past her petite frame. Standing no taller than five feet, Julie's appearance belied the hostility that lurked behind her piercing gaze. Despite the allure of her striking hair, Julie's demeanor was anything but inviting; she seemed to harbor an inexplicable disdain towards me and would occasionally issue veiled threats, casting a shadow of unease over our already tense environment.

Saying, *"I'll get you when we're out of here." "Watch your back because no one else is."* Things like that.

As time went on, things seemed to get worse. Not sure why. One day, I noticed a deck of cards on the table. I innocently took them to my bunk to play solitaire.

In a flash, Julie was screaming at me, saying, *"I'm going to get you; give me back my cards!!"*

I stupidly said, *"They're not your cards; they belong to the jail."*

One of the other women held Julie back, preventing her from coming at me. Julie continued to yell and swear at me. This time, she said she was definitely going to kill me. I was on the bunk; she was near the doorway to the room. Thankfully, the cell door shut suddenly. I was thinking, *"How in the world did that happen? They've never shut before nor been closed."* The door remained closed for a while. Well, it's a good thing they were shut because it gave Julie time to chill out, and it protected me from her.

A jailer came in and reached her arm through the cell bars, saying, *"Vicky, give me the cards."*

I sheepishly walked up to her and handed them over. The jailer said, *"Don't touch the cards for your own sake."*

Julie huffed and said, *"See, they are mine!"* and walked into the other cell room.

After that incident, I always avoided Julie as much as I could, obviously, which was difficult to do in such a small space.

Home away from home

The conditions in what I reluctantly began to call "home" were nothing short of disgusting. The shower, plagued by mold, required a makeshift solution to keep the water running, involving the use of a plastic spoon jammed into the push knob. Despite our efforts, the water flow lasted a mere minute or two, never offering anything beyond lukewarm temperatures. Towels were a rarity, with some inmates resorting to hoarding multiple towels as makeshift pillows. It wasn't until Cindy, a kind soul among us, offered me a towel that I could use for both purposes.

Periodically, the jailers would provide fresh jumpsuits for us to exchange our soiled ones, though some inmates would hoard them in case they weren't replenished. The communal shaver provided for grooming needs was shared among all of us, a practice that bordered on unhygienic. Privacy was a luxury beyond our reach; there were no private toilets, and changing clothes was a public affair. The moldy shower was the only space offering a semblance of seclusion.

Despite the discomfort and occasional indignity, I sought solace in the routine of waking up to the sound of CMT videos blaring from the TV. While the song choices were dictated by two inmates positioned conveniently in front of the TV, the music provided a fleeting sense of freedom, even in the confines of our grim surroundings. However, the constant repetition of songs like "Girl Crush" served as a stark reminder of our confinement and the world beyond the walls.

Description of the jail cell

The conditions in that jail cell were beyond dismal, resembling a scene from a nightmare rather than reality. The once-white walls, now gray and dingy from years of neglect, closed in on us, suffocating any semblance of hope. The stagnant air, tainted with the pungent smell of mold and decay, weighed heavily on our spirits.

The stainless steel toilets, devoid of seats, stood as stark reminders of our loss of dignity and privacy. The faucet, our sole source of water, served dual purposes for both hygiene and hydration, while the scratched and worn-out mirror above the toilet offered distorted reflections of our weary selves.

In the "common" area, the deteriorated table and attached stools bore the scars of countless initials etched into their surfaces, serving as silent witnesses to the passage of time and the transient lives of those who occupied the space.

The cement floor was bare, and the walls were painted gray halfway and dingy white to the ceiling. There were no windows, just a steel door with a small window, which made the cell feel like a dark and dingy box. The bathroom was across from the entrance door of the cell and had no door, offering no privacy. It was dark, cold, wet, and moldy, with a steel toilet and a shower that weakly sprayed lukewarm water. We had to use a plastic spoon to keep the knob in just to run the water, and half the time, it didn't stay.

The cell "bedrooms" were cramped and unwelcoming, each containing a metal bunk equipped with a toilet and a minuscule sink nestled in the corner. The bunks offered little respite, their uncomfortable surfaces serving as reminders of the discomfort that permeated every aspect of our existence within those walls. The attached sink, barely larger than a basin, provided scant relief for our basic hygiene needs, making tasks like washing our faces or brushing our teeth a challenge.

Twelve to eighteen cellmates were crowded in this tiny cell, sleeping on mats on the floor. There was even a pay phone hanging on the wall. I drew a diagram of the cell to show how ridiculous it was. It was difficult to comprehend that we were expected to endure such deplorable conditions day in and day out, our spirits tested by the relentless cruelty of our environment.

Day in, day out

Each day in the jail, we followed the same monotonous routine, beginning with the harsh glare of the lights flickering on to rouse us from our fitful slumber. We would sit in a daze until a jailer appeared, announcing the arrival of breakfast. We would shuffle out into the hallway, grabbing trays of unappetizing food before returning to our cells to consume our meager meal. After a few moments, the jailer would return to collect our trays, marking the end of the morning ritual.

Throughout the day, inmates would engage in various activities to pass the time. Some would socialize, sharing tales of their past or present, while others would play cards or attempt to catch a glimpse of the outside world through the grainy images on the television screen. Amidst these mundane activities, some sought solace in substances, fashioning makeshift pipes to smoke whatever they could find in the bathroom.

Amidst the chaos of daily life in the jail, there were moments of surrealism that defied explanation. One inmate, with a peculiar penchant for the bizarre, would snort coffee powder off her wrist each morning and evening, her strange ritual a testament to the eccentricities that thrived within those walls. Another would resort to creative measures, affixing a maxi pad to the primary camera to garner the attention of the jailers when in need.

For me, each mealtime became a somber affair, as I would barely eat before retreating to my cell to seek refuge in sleep. Depression weighed heavily upon me, casting a shadow over my thoughts and aspirations. It seemed as though this dismal existence would be my reality indefinitely, and I resigned myself to the bleak fate that lay before me.

I would play out in my head over and over again my old boyfriend driving to Kentucky, paying for bail, and taking me back home to Minnesota. I pictured so many scenarios of how it would happen. Each one is better than the last. It kept my mind preoccupied until dinner time or until I dozed off.

When I first found myself trapped in this dreadful place, I clung to a shred of confidence, convinced that my innocence would inevitably lead to my release. Every encounter with a jailer became an opportunity to plead for freedom or, at the very least, a chance to use the phone. Unlike my fellow inmates, who had the means to use the payphone with money from family and friends, I relied on the kindness of the jailers to grant me access to the main telephone at the booking counter.

These precious moments were rare and usually occurred in the evening, when the watchful eyes of the higher-ups were presumably elsewhere. With only one number memorized—the phone of my brother David—I would dial it repeatedly, my heart pounding in my chest as I prayed for him to answer. The disappointment of unanswered calls would often bring me to tears, leaving me devastated and longing for a connection to reality and home.

Talking to David or his wife, Kim, was my lifeline, offering a glimmer of hope amidst the darkness of my confinement. Their reassuring words and unwavering support served as a beacon of comfort in my time of need. However, the uncertainty of whether

David would pick up the phone weighed heavily on me, as these opportunities to reach out were few and far between. Occasionally, a group of us from the cell would be escorted down a dimly lit hallway to a door leading to the outside world. The anticipation and excitement of feeling the sun on my skin and breathing in fresh air were palpable as we stepped into the small outdoor area, enclosed by towering brick walls topped with chain-link fences.

Despite the enclosed space, the sounds of the outdoors were a welcome relief from the constant hum and clatter of the prison. I found a secluded corner, closed my eyes, and took deep breaths as I listened to the birds chirping and cars passing by. A sense of calm washed over me. For a brief moment, I was able to forget where I was and feel a glimmer of joy.

When I felt more assured in my surroundings, I inadvertently found myself entangled in conflicts with fellow inmates. It wasn't my intention to stir trouble; rather, I seemed to attract it, perhaps due to my unmistakable Minnesotan demeanor or my inherent kindness, which appeared out of place in such an environment. Engaging more with my fellow inmates during this time, I must have said or done something to provoke certain individuals.

One afternoon, during our allotted time outside, I stumbled upon a feather. Holding it in my hand, I felt a glimmer of vitality return to me. This simple feather, plucked from a nest nestled in the nook of the building, offered a connection to nature, a reminder of life beyond the confines of the jail. I also discovered a couple of small rocks—a creamy white one, likely quartz, and another dark gray one with a subtle sparkle. They were peculiar finds, yet I cherished them as symbols of freedom and home, keeping them close to me by my bedside.

The gals

Amber-thin, blonde. She was pretty with a kind face. She tried to use a pencil as an eyeliner by wetting the lead. She was the one person I actually struck up a slight friendship with. Her crime was possession of drugs. She was from Middlesboro. She had one child, a daughter, and missed her dearly.

Suzie-miss priss. Know it all, pathological liar. She had an auburn haircut, pixie style, with chubby cheeks and light freckles. She bragged about everything, including the crime she committed. She was annoying to be around.

Julie- short and stalky, maybe 5' tall. She had long black hair down to her butt. Loud and very bossy ruled the cell. Very demanding and mean. Uncontrollable fits of anger. She had a bunch of kids she hadn't seen in a while. Crime - drugs.

Cary - short, straight, thin black hair with large freckles. Strong accent, but not from KY. Gaunt pencil-like figure. She snorted her coffee. I'm not sure about her charges - but she sure helped me later on.

Roxy - pretty and slender, seemed kind, but she wasn't trustworthy. She did say I was pretty once. Many other women came and went; some I never knew their names even though they were there a while too.

Some women would be booked late in the evening and gone the next day. Funny, the girl from Dairy Queen from the beginning of my story ended up in jail, too. She spent a few days there before leaving.

Tidbits

In my quest for something to occupy my mind, I turned to the jailers, asking if there was anything to read or do. They handed me a worn-out book, its cover missing and the last third of its pages absent. Despite its tattered state, I delved into its contents eagerly, reading it cover to cover twice over. The story, set in the 1800s, evoked a sense of nostalgia akin to *"Little House on the Prairie,"* complete with a tender love story woven throughout. Unfortunately, the missing ending left me to conjure my own version of a happily ever after.

The only clothes I owned while in the God-forsaken jail was my bra. It was a simple black sports-like bra, but all stretched out. The rest was the orange jumpsuit to wear. Periodically, we had body checks. We'd line up and, one by one, go into this odd room; it was small and reminded me of a closet. A female jailer would ask us to bare all nearly, bend over, and cough. I guess some folks like to sneak peripherally in. It may be their normal process, but for me, it was just one more thing that traumatized me and probably triggered me.

Two or three inmates were allowed to go out during weekdays to fulfill duties such as cleaning or washing dishes in the kitchen. When I found out about this, I begged to go out to work, too; regrettably, my plea was denied. It became apparent that these privileged inmates were effectively reducing their jail time through such activities. Intrigued by this possibility, I inquired about the prospect of doing the same, only to be informed that the decision rested with the judge. However, I was left without guidance on how to proceed or whom to consult for further clarification. Desperate for a solution, I seized every opportunity to approach the head jailer, expressing my readiness to post bail with funds from my savings account, which regrettably remained inaccessible to me. Despite my persistent efforts, my request went unanswered, leaving me disheartened and uncertain of my options.

Stupid mistake

One day, I must have had more courage because I mentioned the mold on the ceiling and bathroom to a jailer. That was such a bad idea. The jailer's reaction was not what I was expecting or hoping for. I only pointed it out because it wasn't safe for everyone to be breathing in black mold spores. What do I know... Well, the jailer said, *"Ah, so you think that's bad and needs to be taken care of?"*

"Ok, then, you all can clean and scrub." The sighs across the room from almost everyone, with raised eyebrows glaring at me, made me shiver in fear.

The jailer continued, *"Pick up all your mats and stuff and bring it all in the hall; I'll grab cleaning supplies."*

When she left, the inmates muddled under their breaths while they continued to glare at me. One of the inmates, the one that almost attacked me before, yelled, pointing at me, *"You fucking bitch! You did it this time!"*

Another inmate came to me and said, *"You need to shut the Fuck Up, we're going to get you for this."*

Despite my offer to take on the cleaning duties alone, the jailer insisted that everyone pitch in. As we emptied the cell and began the daunting task of scrubbing every surface, I couldn't shake off the fear of the unknown consequences awaiting me. With trepidation, I joined the group effort, unsure of what lay ahead.

Some of my fellow inmates diligently swept and mopped the floor, while others engaged in casual conversation, seemingly unfazed by the situation. As we worked together to sanitize our living space, I kept a low profile, silently hoping to avoid any further conflict.

Although tensions remained high, I was relieved that no one acted on the earlier threats. After completing the cleaning tasks, I retreated to my mat, maintaining a cautious distance from the other inmates, determined to avoid any potential confrontation.

Breakdown

The next day, Julie and a buddy of hers started taunting and threatening me during lunch. I didn't know what to do or say. I felt cornered; I began to freeze and tear up.

The one kind jailer named Heidi opened the cell door, saying, *"Victoria, come with me."* She brought me down the hall; I still had my lunch tray in my hands. She got me outside and said, *"Stay out here."*

Broke down and balled non-stop until I hyperventilated. I couldn't control my sobbing as I sat on the pavement, cradling myself and rocking back and forth. I was so alone, scared, and felt beyond help. I cried out to the Lord, *"Save me, help me out of this place!"* but I thought he didn't hear me.

Was this it? Would I be here forever? I rarely got to talk with my brother, David, and his wife, Kim. They were my only means of reality and hope. I continued to cry while tears stained my shirt.

I began to pray again, saying, *"Lord, you are the only one who can help me; please help me through this."*

As I paced the courtyard, I focused on the soothing sounds of nature surrounding me. The cheerful chirping of house sparrows provided a welcome distraction, while the occasional passing car and the mysterious machine's rhythmic noise filled the air. Despite my initial anxiety, I gradually felt a sense of calm washing over me.

For those precious 20 minutes outdoors, I savored the feeling of freedom, a brief respite from the confines of the jail cell and the oppressive atmosphere within. It was a momentary escape from the presence of other inmates and the tension created by the stern jailers.

When jailor Heidi called me back inside with her gentle southern voice, I reluctantly returned, grateful for her compassionate demeanor amidst the harshness of my surroundings. Her kindness offered a glimmer of hope in an otherwise bleak situation, and I silently vowed to express my gratitude to her someday for her unwavering support.

Passing time

As I drifted in and out of sleep, I found solace in daydreams of my life back home, imagining familiar faces and comforting scenarios. I often wondered about the well-being of elderly acquaintances and longed for the presence of my siblings or an old friend to offer support.

Occasionally, I would engage in conversation with a reserved fellow inmate, finding brief moments of companionship in our shared confinement. On one occasion, we even passed the time with a game of cards, offering a temporary escape from the monotony of our surroundings.

The jail's meager toiletry provisions left much to be desired, with only a basic bar of soap and a small bottle of harsh shampoo provided. However, through the generosity of another inmate, who had managed to obtain Suave shampoo and conditioner, I occasionally indulged in the luxury of softer, more manageable hair. Maintaining a positive rapport with her ensured access to this small but cherished comfort amidst the bleakness of our shared reality.

The jail food was hardly appetizing, consisting mainly of slop, hot dogs, beans, and eggs, among other unappealing items. Occasionally, I would receive a small reprieve in the form of a cookie or brownie accompanying my meal. Unfortunately, I couldn't partake in the snacks like pop, chips, and candy bars that other inmates enjoyed, as I lacked the means to purchase them. My depression only exacerbated my waning appetite, leading me to often leave my meals untouched or forego them entirely.

As the days dragged on, I found myself sinking deeper into despair. Nightly, a jailer would deliver my medication, yet even with its presence, thoughts of death loomed heavy in my mind. What was the purpose of it all? I felt trapped, with no escape from the confines of my reality.

There were nights when falling asleep felt like an impossible task. The cacophony of snoring inmates, reminiscent of chainsaws, filled the air, while the oppressive atmosphere weighed heavily upon me. Tossing and turning offered no respite, prompting me to curl up into a ball, seeking solace in the sanctuary of my thoughts. As I faced the wall, I found refuge in the fairytales spun by my mind, though tears often accompanied my silent reverie.

Days blended into nights as I lay quietly in my bed, enveloped by the suffocating reality of my new "home." Despite the attempts of some inmates to offer encouragement, I found myself surrendering to despair. Alone with my thoughts, I would drift off into fitful slumber, pondering the fate of Sam. My knowledge of him was scant: a resident of the Hibbing area, skilled in guitar, yet bearing the scars of a troubled soul.

"Spending time in jail was my lowest of lows. I didn't see any hope for my future; I felt trapped, alone, and unwanted."

I lift up my eyes to the mountains— where does my help come from? My help comes from the LORD, the Maker of heaven and earth. Psalm 121:1-2

Chapter 29

There is hope

Seriously, I didn't know.

Cary, the girl with the freckles, might have had some peculiar habits like snorting coffee grounds, but her friendly demeanor shone through. Initially, I was unsure about trusting her completely, but as I observed her kindness and helpfulness over time, I began to feel more comfortable around her. Slowly but surely, I realized that she was someone I could rely on and confide in, despite her quirky behavior.

I observed Cary using the payphone one day and couldn't help but be curious about how she managed to make calls. When I asked her, she calmly replied, *"I'm calling my defense attorney. It's free to call him."*

I was taken aback, my mouth hanging open in disbelief.

"Why hadn't I known about this?" I wondered.

It seemed like such crucial information that no one had bothered to share with me. Grateful for her guidance, I pressed her for more details, and she patiently explained the process. It struck me how something so important had been overlooked, leaving me feeling frustrated and wishing I had been informed sooner. None of the inmates, jailers, or even the judge had mentioned this possibility to me.

Even though with Cary's helpful advice, I remained hesitant and incredibly nervous. Ever since my first arrest back in June in Middlesboro, I had felt like I was treated differently. Summoning all my courage, I said a prayer and dialed the number she provided. A kind lady answered and provided me with the necessary information. She assured me that the attorney, Mr. Lee, would be in touch.

"When?" I exclaimed, eagerly hoping today. She said she was uncertain.

Time seemed to crawl by in the jail, each day blending into the next with no sign of progress. I was losing hope when suddenly, the phone rang—one of the few moments of excitement in my monotonous routine. My heart raced as I picked up the receiver, hoping for a glimmer of good news.

It was Mr. Lee on the other end of the line, my appointed public defense attorney. His voice brought a surge of relief as he explained that he had my file and would be representing me in court the following week. Despite the lingering weight of depression and anxiety, his words filled me with a newfound sense of hope. Finally, it seemed like there might be a way out of the darkness. One of the jailers, perhaps sensing my mounting anxiety, granted me the rare privilege of using the main phone to call my brother David. With a pounding heart, I dialed his number, praying for a glimmer of hope in the midst of my turmoil. Thankfully, he picked up, and I eagerly shared the news of my impending court hearing. Despite his reassuring words, the weight of my precarious situation still hung heavy on my shoulders—no money, no ID, no phone, no car. David promised to do what he could to expedite my return to Minnesota, offering a lifeline of hope in the midst of uncertainty.

On the day of my court hearing, every beat of my heart reverberated through my chest like a drum of anticipation. Handcuffed and accompanied by a few other inmates, I was escorted to the courthouse, where we were corralled into a holding room. The atmosphere was charged with nervous energy as each person's name was called, one by one, signaling their moment of reckoning in the courtroom. When my turn came, I was ushered into the hallowed halls of justice, my eyes scanning the room in search of familiar faces. There, amidst the sea of strangers, I caught sight of someone who bore a striking resemblance to Sam, the shadowy figure from my past. His once-dark hair was now bleached blonde, casting doubt on my recognition. Yet, I couldn't shake the feeling that it was him, haunting me like a ghost from a bygone era. My lawyer, Mr. Lee, stood resolutely by my side as we entered the courtroom. With a solemn nod, he instructed me to remain silent, assuring me that he would be my voice in this legal arena. As the judge recited the litany of charges against me—

disorderly conduct, trespassing (twice over), and the alarming accusation of indecent exposure within the confines of the jail—my heart sank with each word uttered. Yet, amidst the looming dread, a glimmer of hope emerged when the judge pronounced my impending release, contingent upon a single stipulation: never to set foot in Bell County again. With a solemn nod, I acquiesced to this condition, grateful for the prospect of freedom but apprehensive about the logistics of retrieving my car from the impound in Middlesboro.

With a decisive gavel strike, my fate was sealed, and Mr. Lee swiftly guided me out of the courtroom, shielding me from the prying eyes of the spectators. Relief washed over me like a gentle tide, tempered by the weight of uncertainty that still lingered in the air. As we ventured into the unknown terrain beyond the courthouse walls, I couldn't help but wonder how I would navigate the final leg of this harrowing journey—reclaiming my semblance of normalcy amidst the remnants of chaos and despair.

The evening prior, during a heartfelt conversation with my brother David and sister-in-law Kim, I received a glimmer of hope amid the darkness of uncertainty. They relayed the astonishing news that one of the Appalachian fellows I had once shared hunting expeditions with had generously covered the expenses to retrieve my impounded car. David, ever the steadfast pillar of support, had also arranged for funds to be wired to me at the local Walmart in

Middlesboro, ensuring I had the means to fuel my journey homeward.

In the midst of grappling with the practicalities of my impending release, Kim offered a practical suggestion that resonated deeply—acquiring a budget-friendly track phone to bridge the communication gap that had plagued me throughout this ordeal. Their unwavering support and thoughtful gestures served as a beacon of light in the midst of my tumultuous journey, instilling within me a renewed sense of resilience and determination to overcome the obstacles that lay ahead.

"All that time, I didn't know I could get a lawyer, nor did anyone tell me. Maybe I was meant to be there for that period of time for lamenting."

Out of the depths, I cry to you, O Lord, Lord, hear my voice! - Psalm 130:1

Chapter 30

Minnesota Bond

Relief

Mr. Lee kindly offered me a ride to Middlesboro, which I gratefully accepted. Throughout the journey, I remained mostly silent, expressing my gratitude intermittently. Upon arriving at Joe's towing, I hesitantly knocked on the door, hoping for a swift resolution. However, my anxiety mounted as no one answered my call. With each passing moment, my apprehension grew, fearing another encounter with law enforcement. After what felt like an eternity, a figure emerged from the back of the building - Joe, the owner. With a sense of relief washing over me, I received my keys from him, eager to put this chapter behind me.

He said, *"Your vehicle stinks."*

"Yep, there was a fish in there," I said.

He continued, recounting how one of his employees stumbled upon the stench weeks after my car had been towed. It was discovered that the rotting fish had been concealed within a pant leg. Feeling a mix of embarrassment and amusement, I offered a sheepish smile as I listened to his story. After expressing my gratitude to Mr. Lee, I hopped into my car and headed straight for Walmart, eager to address the pressing matters at hand. While at Walmart, I walked right to customer service, stating the money was wired to me. She looked up my name and the information and said, *"No, sorry dear, not here."*

"That can't be," I exclaimed. *"Please check again."* She said she would, but it would take a moment. I ran back to my car, sitting and praying. I looked in my overhead mirror and said, *"Ew, my eyebrows!"*

After months of neglect, I decided it was high time to address my grooming routine. Armed with my makeup bag, I embarked on a plucking session to tidy up my appearance. Once satisfied with the results, I returned to the task at hand to get the money wired to me. I anxiously waited as the customer service rep; handed me the money. Without hesitation, I made a beeline for the essentials - a track phone, a refreshing Coke, a Snickers bar, and some nacho Bugles. It had been far too long since I indulged in these simple pleasures.

Snacks in hand, ready to 'get the heck' out of here, I jumped in my stinky Chevy. Traveling north on Highway 25E, leaving Pineville behind, felt like a weight lifted off my shoulders. Making calls to my siblings, letting them know I was on my way back to Minnesota, brought much relief. Fortunately, my brother Greg offered me a place to stay in Illinois. Understandably, the memories of those days with Greg and his family are a bit hazy, given everything I've been through. I do recall, though, a powerful song

Greg shared with me 'Deliverer' by Matt Maher. The lyrics resonated with me and still do to this day.

Finding a stable place to stay with my sister Roseann in Minneapolis was a welcome relief after facing homelessness and uncertainty. The date of my arrival, August 6th, 2015, marked the beginning of a new chapter in my journey. However, the realization that my dad's rifle was missing from my vehicle was distressing, especially considering its sentimental value. It's disheartening to think that items like my gold cross necklace, sapphire white gold ring, and Visa gift card were also not returned to me after my release from jail. It seems that my time in Kentucky brought not only emotional turmoil but also the loss of valuable possessions, adding to the challenges I faced during that period.

"I was so determined to get out of the area and get back to Minnesota. During my drive, I cried off and on in a state of relief."

Tears of joy will stream down their faces, and I will lead them home with great care. They will walk beside quiet streams and on smooth paths where they will not stumble. - Jeremiah 31:9

Chapter 31

'Sifting through the ashes'

Kangas and a job

As the weight of my loneliness grew heavier each day, I found myself reaching out to Kangas, hoping to hear the familiar warmth in his voice. Our nightly phone calls became a fragile thread connecting me to a semblance of comfort. His words felt like a lifeline amid the cold isolation that surrounded me. Though my sister was kind enough to take me in, I didn't have a proper bedroom. Instead, I made do with a simple mattress tucked away in the dimly lit lower level.

The darkness of the room felt suffocating, as if it mirrored the bleakness that settled into my soul. Days blurred into nights, and it seemed as though the light had abandoned me, leaving me to navigate the shadows alone. Each morning, I'd wake to the same heavy grayness, wondering if there would ever be an escape from the suffocating darkness.

Recognizing that I desperately needed a job, I submitted applications to various social services positions, hoping something would come through. After a period of nervous anticipation, I was finally offered a position as a program director in September, which was a huge relief. However, there was a catch: the job was on the

South end of the Twin Cities, quite a distance from my sister's place. This meant I would need to find a new home closer to work. Fortunately, my friend Kangas was also in the process of relocating, and we decided to join forces to find a townhome that was conveniently located between our jobs. After much searching and comparing options, we finally found a townhome that met our needs, providing both of us with a sense of stability and relief as we settled into our new environment.

The depression weighed heavily on me, suffocating me like a thick fog. It felt just like it had in 2011—crippling, all-consuming, leaving me feeling lost and disconnected from the world. I desperately wanted to sleep away the shame and embarrassment caused by my manic episodes. Life had become an endless abyss of despair, with each day seeming like an impossible struggle. Every day, bleakness grew in my heart, but I pushed myself to work hard at my new job. It gave me a sense of normalcy amidst the chaos of my life. The routine and purpose it provided were my only solace in an otherwise tumultuous existence.

Counseling

I began attending Christian counseling sessions with a counselor named Sheila Marker. During our discussions, Sheila suggested that I consider Eye Movement Desensitization and Reprocessing (EMDR) therapy to address the trauma and the manic episodes I'd recently experienced. The key idea behind EMDR is that traumatic experiences can create blockages in the brain's processing system. These blockages can lead to persistent negative thoughts, feelings, and behaviors, causing distress and impacting everyday life. EMDR aims to unlock these blockages by using bilateral stimulation—such as eye movements, tapping, or auditory cues—while focusing on specific traumatic memories.

Sheila mentioned that I exhibited signs of Post-Traumatic Stress Disorder (PTSD) in addition to my bipolar diagnosis. When she said that, it was like a lightbulb went off in my head; I could see how much trauma had affected my life. I could also understand how EMDR could potentially help by allowing me to reprocess those difficult memories.

EMDR's impact on a person's life can be profound. It can lead to a significant reduction in symptoms of PTSD, such as flashbacks, anxiety, and hypervigilance. Individuals who undergo EMDR often report improved mood, better sleep, reduced feelings of fear or guilt, and an overall enhanced sense of well-being. Knowing this, I was hopeful that EMDR could be the key to overcoming the emotional weight I carried from my past.

It was a journey I was willing to take, no matter how challenging it might be, because I knew the outcome could be life-changing. I wanted to be free of the trauma, the emotional triggers, and the sense of being trapped in a cycle of distress. With Sheila's guidance, I began the process, trusting that EMDR could help me find a path to healing and a brighter future.

Pieces of me

In the meanwhile, Kangas kindly offered to assist me in retrieving my belongings from the Iron Range. As we made our way to my old house, where I had left a considerable amount of my possessions, I couldn't help but feel apprehensive. Memories of the past flooded my mind as I knocked on the door.

A lady answered and said, *"You didn't come back, so I got rid of it all."*

Her words caught me off guard, and I was left speechless, unable to comprehend how she could have disposed of my belongings. I reminded her of our agreement and the fact that she had signed it, hoping that it would make a difference. However, she merely shrugged and replied, *"You didn't come back."*

I bolted toward Kangas's truck, tears streaming down my face. My sobs grew louder with each step, as if the sadness was being wrenched from the deepest parts of me. The overwhelming sense of loss hit me like a wave, as if the manic episodes had once again taken something precious from me. I couldn't control my breathing; it came in short, desperate gasps as I fell into Kangas's arms. The garage was filled with all my things—items I cherished, the art supplies that had once been my refuge, the clothes that held memories of better times, and other pieces of my past. Now, it felt like all of it was slipping away.

Despite Kangas's attempts to comfort me, I was inconsolable. I couldn't stop the tears; they fell like rain, a torrent of grief and anger that I couldn't contain. It felt as if my world had been dismantled, piece by piece, until there was nothing left but a hollow shell. My world, once vibrant and full of potential, now felt empty. I was hyperventilating, and it grew worse as my mind raced, trying to comprehend what had happened and why it always felt like everything I cared about was being taken away.

As we drove away, I felt a growing sense of unease. The uncertainty about the fate of my belongings at Sam's dad's place gnawed at me. What if they weren't there anymore? What if everything I valued had vanished? The more I thought about it, the more anxious I became. I suggested to Kangas that we head over there, hoping against hope that my fears were unfounded.

When we arrived, I made a beeline for the shed where my boxes were stored. The anticipation was like a tight knot in my stomach. I opened the door, holding my breath as I peeked inside. A wave of relief washed over me as I saw my boxes stacked neatly, just as I'd left them. They were still there, untouched and intact.

As I sifted through the boxes, my hands trembled with a mix of anxiety and relief. There were the family pictures, snapshots of my childhood, and my parents' wedding album— these were irreplaceable memories, pieces of my life that I thought I had lost forever. I found my framed artwork, the pieces I had poured my heart into. I couldn't stop the tears that welled up in my eyes, but these were tears of gratitude. My emotions spilled over as I realized how lucky I was to have recovered these precious mementos.

I took a deep breath, feeling the tightness in my chest loosen. Despite all the chaos and upheaval, I was blessed enough to reclaim these tokens of my past. It was as if I was reclaiming a part of myself, a part I thought I'd never see again. This moment of thankfulness amidst the turmoil was a much-needed reminder that sometimes, just sometimes, things turn out okay.

I made my way to the temporary apartment complex where I was supposed to live and arrived at my old apartment door, where I knocked to retrieve my belongings. The people who were currently occupying the apartment had my bed, art desk, and purple desk chair, but they graciously allowed me to retrieve my art desk and chair once I explained my circumstances.

As soon as I stepped out of the apartment, I was met with a barrage of angry voices from people who knew me. They were yelling and swearing, accusing me of stealing things that belonged to the apartment's current occupants. My friend Kangas and I ignored their accusations and quickly loaded my desk and chair into our trailer.

Finally, we arrived at the townhome we rented, which was a beautiful and spacious living space. Kangas had generously paid for all of the furniture since he was able to afford it. Despite this, I still wanted to make the space feel personal, so I hung up my artwork on the walls to give the townhome a touch of my own style.

"During this period, I dealt with some horrendous painful emotions that wreaked havoc on me."

I hold fast to your statutes, LORD; do not let me be put to shame. Psalm 119:31

Chapter 32

Puppy

Border Collie

As I thought about getting a puppy again, my heart filled with joy. I missed Bo and the comfort of having a furry friend around. After some contemplation, I started toying with the idea of getting a border collie—those prick ears and sleek coats had always been adorable to me, and their intelligence was truly impressive.

When I stumbled upon a website with a border collie pup for sale, it felt like fate. I had been browsing online, looking at dog breeds and checking local animal shelters, hoping to find a puppy to bring some joy back into my life. Excited at the prospect of finally having a new companion, I asked Kangas to accompany me to pick up the pup. However, when I called the seller, my heart sank as she informed me that the pup had already been sold. Disappointed, I couldn't help but cry, feeling as though I had lost my chance at finding happiness. It was as if my hopes had been snatched away, leaving me feeling alone and heartbroken.

Just when I thought my heart couldn't sink any lower, the seller offered a glimmer of hope. She mentioned that her friend had a litter of Border Collie puppies and gave me the contact details.

My spirits lifted, and I hurried to tell Kangas. We set off immediately, driving with renewed excitement. When we arrived, the puppies were playing in the yard, a tumble of black and white fur. It was the most adorable sight, each pup with its own unique markings and playful personality. But my eyes locked onto a particular one—a male pup with a coat as black as midnight, a striking white belly, and a splash of brown on his right front leg. He bounded toward me with an infectious energy, and I instantly knew that he was the one for me. The disappointment I had felt earlier melted away, replaced with a sense of joy and connection. My search for companionship had ended, and a new adventure with this little guy was about to begin.

On the drive back home, I held the pup close, feeling his warmth and comfort. That night, I slept on the recliner with him snuggled safely in my arms. As I watched him sleep, I thought about what to call him. When I asked Kangas for suggestions, he quickly exclaimed, *"Cooper!"* The name seemed perfect, and it stuck.

Cooper soon became my pride and joy, bringing light to even my darkest days. We went on long walks together, visited dog parks, and even went to work together. His presence was therapeutic, and he brought a smile to everyone he met. With Cooper by my side, life was brighter, and my heart was full of love. He truly became my sunshine through the rain. Even after all these years, Cooper has a remarkable ability to sense when I need a comforting hug, and his silly antics never fail to make me laugh. He's always by my side, loyal and loving, and I know that I can count on him whenever I need him most.

"Dogs have been a part of my life,
helping me through challenging times.
Cooper is one exceptional dog who hugs me when I need it most.
It's as if he feels my pain."

But ask the animals, and they will teach you, or the birds in the sky, and they will tell you; or speak to the earth, and it will teach you; or let the fish in the sea inform you. Which of all these does not know that the hand of the LORD has done this? In his hand is the life of every creature and the breath of all mankind. Job 12:7-10

Cooper, 10 Weeks Old

Chapter 33

Breakthrough

The Final Turning Point

Despite my best efforts, I found myself struggling to keep up with the demands of my job as a Program Director. I also struggled with a deep depression. However, I was determined to find some solace in my personal life and began searching for a good church in the area.

One day, as I was walking down the street from my townhome, I spotted a non-denominational church that caught my eye. Curious, I decided to attend a service and was pleasantly surprised at what I discovered. The church was filled with warm and welcoming people who immediately made me feel at home. The sermons were thought-provoking and inspiring, and I left feeling a sense of connection. Over time, I began to form deep and meaningful relationships with the members of the church community, and I knew that I had found a place where I truly belonged.

I would put on a smile any time I was near others at work or church, but when it came time for counseling, all walls came down. Depression loomed over me day and night. I'd pray all the time for freedom from the depression. I spent time reading the bible, but I didn't talk about the mania or depression with others except my family. I was so afraid of being judged for my mental illness. I have lost so many friends and been judged by many people, including Christians, for being mentally ill.

I prayed so much for freedom from the depression. I journaled often as well. I would play worship music to soothe my soul and praise Jesus through this dark time. I'd have glimmers of joy, but it would fade quickly back to the bleak, dark depression.

On my birthday, April 12th, 2016, I wrote in my journal a prayer to the Lord-

The only thing I want today as a birthday gift is complete freedom and deliverance. To have total joy, no anxiety, no fear, no depression, no PTSD, good memory. To be whole again. To laugh as I laughed, to be happy and free. To help others who go through difficulties. To be what they need, to share my testimony with others. Nothing is impossible with God Luke 1:37. Remain in me, and I will remain in you John 15:4. Joy made complete in Him John 15:11, Ask me anything in my name, and I will do it. John 14:14. Tears all day long, anger built up. I CAN'T DO THIS ANYMORE! I CAN'T, JESUS. PLEASE TAKE THIS BURDEN. I thank you, I praise you, I seek you, I read your word. I ask for prayer, and I go to counseling. I do what I can.

I didn't go to work that day. Instead, all day, I slept or cried lying in bed, Cooper by my side. I continued to cry out to the Lord to deliver me, to help me, to free me. *"Lord, please, all I want is to not deal with mental illness. Please remove this burden from me."*

April 14th, 2016, I journaled-

Cast ALL anxiety and worry on God because He cares! –

1 Peter 5:7

A new day, a fresh start. No fear, trust in Him, wait and see as He makes all things new. Yesterday is gone - gone. Remember that. It is gone, finished; press in and see it is a new day; keep pressing in, and don't give up! Give thanks in spite of difficult circumstances.

– Philippians 4:6

Sense God's comfort and hope, -

2 Thessalonians 2:16

April 15th, 2016 –

The second day, I woke anxiety-free. Yesterday was calm, peaceful, and easy. Today is starting that way. Each day I journaled, every word I wrote was positive and exclaiming freedom from depression, anxiety, and PTSD.

I was free! I asked for this, and I had a breakthrough. I also continued to pray. "Lord, please, I can't handle the horrific events of what bipolar does to me. I would rather die than be bipolar again. Please, please, Lord, take this burden; may I never be like that again."

Celebrating my birthday in 2016 marked the beginning of a new chapter in my life, one that I never could have anticipated. It was a year of transformation and growth, all thanks to my newfound connection with Bridgewood Church. The community there not only welcomed me but also offered countless opportunities for personal growth and adventure. Joining the church turned out to be a pivotal moment that reshaped my journey in the most unexpected and joyful ways.

One of the most life-changing experiences came from participating in two mission trips to Tala, Kenya, in December 2016 and December 2017. These trips were more than just travel; they were gateways to experiencing a vibrant new culture, meeting remarkable people, and creating lasting memories. I found myself immersed in the warmth and beauty of Kenya, where I forged connections that transcended borders and languages.

In December 2016, while I was in Kenya, a young man named Kennedy Lukoye shared a dream he had about going to the United States. In his dream, he saw fog, a river, and big cities, but he couldn't seem to reach his destination. I chuckled and told him that his dream reminded me of Minneapolis/St. Paul, Minnesota, where the Mississippi River runs through the cities and there is sometimes fog. We both laughed and smiled.

I encouraged Kennedy, telling him that if he was meant to come to the USA, God would provide a way, and I promised to help him with the process. Kennedy worked hard to obtain a student visa to attend Concordia in St. Paul, MN, and I helped him find a place to live with a family from Bridgewood church.

Today, Kennedy lives in Minnesota with his wife and baby girl. He has finished his master's degree and even wrote his own memoir called The Case for Resilience. It's amazing to see how God moves mountains and uses us as instruments to help others.

Beyond the mission trips, the church itself became a sanctuary where I built meaningful relationships and discovered a newfound sense of belonging. The supportive community helped me find a new place to live, a significant upgrade from my previous circumstances living with Kangas. It was as if everything started to align, bringing a sense of harmony and abundance into my life.

In short, those years have been nothing short of a miracle. I feel blessed to have found a church that welcomed me with open arms and provided me with the guidance and support I needed to thrive.

Sexuality

Life went well for some time, with a stable job, supportive friends, and a comfortable lifestyle. However, there was a gnawing emptiness that persisted – a deeply felt need for a healthy and fulfilling romantic relationship. Despite going out on dates and meeting new people, nothing ever seemed to click. By 2017, I hit a breaking point and decided to give up on relationships altogether. It felt like I was cursed to either meet the wrong men or sabotage any potential for a real connection. Overwhelmed by the weight of unfulfilled longing for companionship and love, I remember crying out to God in desperation. I even had one relationship where I slapped the man in the face for what he said. I called the police after he physically assaulted me. Still, I am the one who went to jail over the weekend because I initiated the fight. Boy, I needed to learn my lesson. *No more men,* I thought.

I always thought my relationships failed because of something I did wrong—maybe it was my personality or my bipolar disorder. I would beat myself up every time someone walked away, replaying the moments, dissecting every conversation, trying to figure out what I'd done to push them away. But no matter how much I tried to rationalize it, I always felt this gnawing emptiness.

It wasn't until I spent hours praying and pouring my heart out into my journal that I began to understand what was really happening. The damage wasn't from something recent—it was deep, old, and painful. Inside me was a little girl who had been shattered long ago, a girl whose innocence was stolen before she could even understand what it meant. The trauma of my childhood and early adulthood, the things I endured but never spoke of, had left me with scars that never healed.

I had buried the pain, hidden it beneath layers of forced smiles and laughter, pretending it didn't exist. But it was always there, lurking in the shadows, affecting my every interaction, my every relationship. It wasn't my fault that things fell apart—I was carrying a burden I didn't even know was there. As I started to face the truth, to acknowledge the trauma, I realized that healing wouldn't come from blaming myself. It would come from accepting the past, no matter how painful, and finding a way to move forward.

"It was for freedom that Christ has set me free," I'd remind myself. But even with those words echoing in my heart, I couldn't shake the feeling of being trapped. The Bible says there's no condemnation for those in Christ Jesus, yet I felt weighed down by guilt, as if invisible chains bound me. The shadows of the past were long, and they stretched across my soul.

The roots of my struggle went deep. They started with the unspeakable damage from my childhood and teen years when I was abused. Those awful events, which I spent years trying to forget, shaped the way I understood sex and love. They left scars that seemed to twist my view of relationships, intimacy, and even my own worth.

But it wasn't just the memories that haunted me—it was the pattern of sexual sin they led to. The same darkness that stole my innocence left me vulnerable to the same cycle of pain and guilt. I felt caught in a loop, unable to break free.

299

Thankfully, with time and through the gentle guidance of counseling, I began to find my way out. It was a slow process, but healing came, even to the deepest parts of my soul. The journey wasn't easy, but step by step, I found release from the torment of sexual abuse and the sin that followed. The day came when I could finally believe that I wasn't condemned, that I was forgiven, and that I was truly free.

I experienced a profound shift within my being as I felt the loving presence of the Lord healing the deep wounds that had weighed so heavily on my soul for far too long. Each passing moment seemed to bring a gentle yet powerful force that worked quietly but relentlessly, chipping away at the remnants of trauma that had left me feeling broken and fragmented. It was as if the Lord was carefully putting the pieces of my heart back together, one by one, until I began to feel a newfound sense of wholeness and peace.

Through this transformative process, I was reminded that when we open ourselves to His love and healing, the possibilities are limitless. The burden of my past traumas began to lift, replaced by the gentle warmth of hope. For the first time in a long while, I felt that my life could be different—that I could be free from the chains that had bound me. It was a remarkable journey, filled with moments of deep reflection, prayer, and quiet tears of gratitude. In those moments, I knew that with the Lord's touch, my soul was finding its way back to a place of light and healing.

"Wow, the depression lifted, finally.
The Lord gave me my birthday gift.
I am forever grateful.
He healed me of the wounds deepest in my heart."

I am the Lord who heals you. Exodus 15:26

Chapter 34

A Date Changed Everything

The Farmer

I had created a profile on a dating site, but I had stopped using it actively. My profile stated, *"I love Jesus; I am Christian. Don't bother messaging me unless you love Him too."*

However, just before Christmas in 2017, an unexpected message from a man named Craig Stehr caught my attention. He introduced himself and said that he loved the Lord and that he would like to call me.

Craig and I had chatted a few times and agreed to meet up. He suggested Stark's, a nearby restaurant known for its good food and lively dance floor, making it ideal for a dinner and dance date. I had always been a fan of dancing, especially the two-step, which my uncle taught me when I was younger. I had always hoped to find someone who loved dancing as much as I did, and it seemed like Craig might be that person.

On the date, Craig was very outgoing and talkative, filling me in on his kids and his farm. He had a lot to say, but his stories were interesting, and his warmth was infectious. I could see his enthusiasm and knew he was someone with a good heart. Although he did most of the talking, I didn't mind listening to his tales. I was just glad to be with someone who was so open and genuine. It felt like we had known each other for much longer than just a few conversations.

After dinner, Craig took me by the hand and said, *"Let's go dance."* As we waltzed around the dance floor, he showed me his impressive two-step and waltzing skills. I felt like I was floating on air as he held me close with his strong hands. There was something about Craig that was different from anyone I had ever met before. I did not feel like I had a crush on him, nor did I feel like I had to impress him. He was humble and kind, and I felt safe and comfortable with him.

Craig and I enjoyed our conversations so much that he made a point of calling me every day, which made me feel exceptional. I felt special, and he made a point of proving it to me with each day, every minute. He shared things about his life, about his farm, where he raised some extraordinary Angus cows and calves. Intrigued, I accepted his invitation to visit his farm and see it all for myself.

As soon as I arrived, Craig welcomed me with open arms and showed me around his beautiful property. The cows were all lying on the corn stalk bedding during the cold January weather. The smell of hay and corn silage filled the air. I never thought that I could ever think of a cattle yard as beautiful. Craig's presence made me see things in a different light. Craig then took me through his daily farm chores, which included feeding and herding the cows. Watching him work with such passion and expertise was a true delight. His commitment to his duty was infectious. I left Craig's farm with a newfound appreciation for the hard work and dedication that goes into farming.

When Craig introduced me to his three children- Ryan, Alyssa, and Derek, I was immediately struck by their kindness, attractiveness, and intelligence. Each of them had their own unique qualities and personalities, making them interesting to be around. They were all at different stages in life, whether in college or building their careers. Being with Craig's family, I felt a welcoming sense of warmth and hospitality that was both inviting and comforting.

Craig had a way of engaging with his children that showed he was a loving father. His genuine interest in their lives and his effortless conversations with them gave me a glimpse into the strong bonds they shared. It wasn't long before I started to feel like I belonged in their family. Spending time with Craig and his kids made me feel more at ease than I had in a long time, and I began to look forward to our future together with a newfound sense of excitement and hope.

Craig and I set out on a quest to find the perfect horses at a nearby auction. The excitement of bidding on horses that could potentially become my new companions was exhilarating. As we walked through the rows of horses, I carefully observed each one, hoping to find the perfect partner. Although I had never purchased a horse from an auction before, I was eager to find some quality horses.

As I watched the arena, I noticed a talented palomino mare named Ruby. She was a gorgeous double-registered quarter horse, ten years old, and had impressive skills such as rollbacks, and side passes. My heart raced as I put in my bid. I was thrilled when the other bidder dropped out, and I was able to purchase her.

Meanwhile, Craig was watching an older man ride a large red dun mare. He was mesmerized by her slow and steady movements, and he knew that she would be the perfect match for him. After some convincing, I decided to bid on the mare, and I ended up buying her too. She is an 11-year-old registered red dun quarter horse mare named Cindy.

After bringing the mares to Craig's farm, we gave them time to rest and adjust to their new surroundings. When the time came, we hauled them to Haycreek, just 15 miles away. We saddled them up and went for a ride on the breathtaking trails hidden in the bluffs. The picturesque view of the countryside, the sound of the rustling leaves, and the gentle clip-clop of the horses' hooves made for a perfect day. As we rode, I couldn't help but feel grateful for Craig's willingness to ride a horse. He called horses his *new hobby.'*

I vividly remember the times when I used to wish that I could find a boyfriend who would be willing to ride a horse with me. But it seemed like an impossible dream until I met Craig. He was different, and every day, he was winning more and more points in my book. What I loved most about him was that he always made me feel special. He would buy me flowers not only for special occasions but even when I would come to visit. The sight of him with a bouquet of fresh flowers in his hand would brighten up my day and make me feel loved. It was these little things that made me fall for him, and I knew that I had found someone special.

Craig and I found a great church in Red Wing, New River Assemblies of God, which felt like home from the very first visit. The sermons were insightful, diving deep into faith and the Bible, and the worship was genuinely uplifting. Craig often remarked that he had never felt more connected to his spirituality than at this church, where every message seemed to resonate with him.

On a lovely summer day in August 2019, Craig and I decided to ride our horses in Haycreek. However, the day didn't start off as planned. I was in a foul mood, and while tacking up, I accidentally hit my head, causing tears to well up in my eyes. The frustration from the morning, combined with the pain from my head injury, made me feel like this was not the ideal day for a ride. Despite the rough start, Craig's comforting presence and patience helped me through it, offering support and understanding when I needed it most. Craig consoled me and said, *"Come on, let's walk the horse over there by the trailhead before we mount the horses."*

We walked the horses to the trailhead by the picnic tables. The trail was lined with tall grass full of blooming daisies.

Craig on Cindy, me on Ruby 2019 after he proposed

Craig got down on one knee and held a beautiful colossal diamond ring in his hand, saying, *"Will you marry me, a farmer?"* The moment was so unexpected that I burst into tears, overwhelmed with joy and disbelief. I couldn't speak for a few seconds, just staring at him, but when I found my voice, I said, "*Yes!*" throwing my arms around him in a tight hug.

A few months later, on November 19th, 2019, Craig and I said our vows in a simple, intimate ceremony surrounded by close family and friends. The day was a picture-perfect autumn scene. I wore a stunning lace gown, perfectly complemented by my favorite cowboy boots, while Craig looked dashing in his crisp white shirt and a classic velvet vest. Our families joined in our celebration, creating a warm and welcoming atmosphere. It was a day filled with love, joy, and the beginning of a new chapter in our lives. We couldn't have asked for a more beautiful start to our journey together.

After the ceremony, we had a small gathering at Starks, the place where Craig and I first met. It was a joyous occasion filled with laughter, love, some timeless two-step dancing and waltzing.

Craig, the hardworking farmer, has become an integral part of my life. He is my rock, my best friend, and my true love. Every day, I feel blessed to have him by my side.

I'm eternally grateful to Craig and his family for their love and support. I had spent nine long years dating the wrong people before meeting Craig, and I never thought I would find true love. But with Craig, I feel complete, and I know that I'm exactly where I'm meant to be.

Children

As a young girl, I had a very active imagination, and I used to spend hours dreaming about my future, which always included having my own children. I often pictured myself having twin babies, a boy, and a girl, that I would dote on and cherish. However, when I married Scott, we agreed we wouldn't have children. Despite my attempts to accept this decision, the longing for children never truly faded. It was a long and difficult battle, but I eventually came to the realization that it would be best never to have children. I didn't want to put a child through the turmoil of having a mentally ill mother like me.

Even with this realization, the Lord had plans to bless me in unexpected ways. Craig, my second husband, had three adult children, and though they weren't my own, I grew to love them as if they were. When Craig's eldest son had a baby, I became a grandmother. The moment I held that little one in my arms, I was overwhelmed with joy and a deep sense of belonging. I knew that I would love and support her unconditionally, just like I did with her father. I know there will be more grandchildren to come, and I can't wait to shower them with love and affection. I am grateful for the blessings that I have received and cherish every moment with my extended family.

Puppy's

Cooper, who had become a farm dog, needed a companion. So, Craig and I got an older puppy named Patches from my brother David. We decided to breed Patches with a handsome and friendly blue merle border collie named Oakley. The process of having puppies brought me immense joy, even though I was somewhat nervous due to the previous experience with Gracie from years back. Finally, the day arrived when Patches went into labor. I lost sleep worrying, but in the end, Patches gave birth to seven beautiful puppies. I am incredibly grateful to have had the opportunity to breed and raise puppies again, just like in the old days with my dad.

I truly believe the Lord takes situations in our lives,
regardless if they weren't a part of His will
and intertwines them
into His beautiful perfect plan."

And the God of all grace, who called you to his eternal glory in Christ, after you have suffered a little while, will himself restore you and make you strong, firm, and steadfast. 1 Peter 5:10

Chapter 35

Who I Am

Freedom

I've reached a point in my life where I refuse to let bipolar disorder define me. It's no longer the lens through which I see my entire existence. Instead, I've chosen to focus on the things that make me whole and the steps I need to take to stay grounded and strong. It's not about denying my condition—it's about acknowledging it without allowing it to overshadow everything else. As a psychiatrist once said to me, "Bipolar can go into remission if you haven't had any manic or depressive episodes." I haven't had any episodes since the depression lifted after my birthday in 2016. I am truly thankful and amazed I have been bipolar episode-free for many years. I am determined to maintain my mental, emotional, and spiritual health.

I am committed to taking the necessary steps to ensure that I am in a good place, even if it means facing difficult truths or taking uncomfortable actions. This requires constant effort and vigilance. But I've come to accept that it's worth it to live a fulfilling life. I have been through the turmoil of this disorder, and now I'm ready to focus on the beauty and possibilities that still lie ahead.

After years of experimenting with various medications for bipolar disorder, Lithium and Depakote have proven to be the most effective for me. Yet even with these medications, blood tests show that they barely reach a therapeutic level. Despite this, I remain committed to taking them because they offer a glimpse of stability and control.

To further investigate my condition, I underwent lab tests, which revealed that I had a deficiency in melatonin, a hormone that regulates sleep. To address this, I now supplement my regimen with melatonin and the herb lemon balm, a combination that has helped me get the rest I desperately needed. I'm incredibly grateful for these natural sleep aids, especially since I have experienced many sleepless nights that caused significant turmoil in my life.

Throughout my life, I have yearned to feel the liberation that comes with being healed and delivered from bipolar disorder. I spent countless nights praying for a miracle, hoping for relief from the chaos that once engulfed me. By the grace of Jesus, I have been delivered from those dark times. The deep emotional wounds that once kept me trapped in a cycle of despair have been healed, allowing me to break free from the shadows of my past.

As I embrace this newfound sense of freedom, I can't help but feel a surge of hope and optimism for the future. No longer shackled by the turmoil that once dictated my life, I'm now able to focus on building a life filled with joy, peace, and purpose. It's a profound transformation, one that fills me with gratitude each day as I look forward to a brighter tomorrow. Years ago, I wrote a poem while working with teenagers who struggled with mental illnesses and trauma. I thought of them while writing the poem. I now see that I wrote the poem about myself. I carefully stenciled the poem around a drawing of a rose I drew. It's hanging on my bedroom wall. The poem: *Thorns of protection against this world's deceit, each petal so precious and meek. This rose can only grow from its caretakers' delight, from patience to trust. It will be a sight.* This poem signifies the delicate nature of myself, which requires careful nurturing and protection. I see myself in the rose, fragile but with the strength to protect myself when necessary and reliant on the guidance and protection of the Lord.

During the turbulent times of my life, I felt like I was in pandemonium, but I found solace in the presence of Jesus, who was always by my side, even when I didn't recognize it. The journey of my life was filled with traumas, trials, thrills, and brokenness, but I realized that they were all part of my personal growth. God took the chaos of my life and transformed it into His peace, which gave me the strength to face every obstacle.

I am immensely grateful for Jesus, who I wholeheartedly believe has saved my life countless times. Time and again, I have witnessed inexplicable miracles in my life, or I have been shielded from devastating calamities because of His infinite mercy. Although I may never fully fathom the depth of His wisdom, I know that His ways are always perfect, unwavering

313

compassionate, affectionate, and imbued with true understanding. In every circumstance, He has upheld me and lavished me with unconditional love. Despite my many struggles and mistakes, His mercy endures forever, offering me hope and redemption when I need it most.

Over the years, I have developed a strong passion for assisting individuals dealing with mental illness, addictions, and other life challenges. My extensive experience in social services led me to envision a business that could make a meaningful difference in the lives of those in need. After obtaining the necessary licensing from the state of Minnesota, I set out to establish a social services business dedicated to supporting individuals with disabilities, particularly those affected by mental illness. I am overjoyed to see God's hand in this journey and am amazed by the opportunities that God has opened up for me.

When we are devoted to His word and listen to His plans, great things happen as we overcome the trials of this life! Victory always wins!

"The mania of my past brought me to my present.
I am grateful for enduring these hardships,
regardless of why or how they occurred.
Persevering through built character
through the hope of my redeeming Savior Jesus Christ."

For everyone who has been born of God overcomes the world. And this is the victory that has overcome the world-our faith. 1 John 5:4

PSALM 136

HIS MERCY ENDURES FOREVER

Give thanks to the LORD, for he is good. For his mercy endures forever.

Give thanks to the God of Gods. For his mercy endures forever.

Give thanks to the Lord of Lords. For his mercy endures forever.

To him who alone does great wonders—[a] For his mercy endures forever.

To him who by his understanding made the heavens— For his mercy endures forever.

To him who spread out the earth on the waters— For his mercy endures forever.

To him who made the great lights, For his mercy endures forever.

the sun to rule by day,

the moon and stars to rule by night— For his mercy endures forever.

To him who struck Egypt by killing their firstborn,

For his mercy endures forever.

and brought Israel out from their midst,

with a mighty hand and outstretched arm—

To him who cut the Red Sea in two,

and brought Israel through the middle of it, For his mercy endures
forever.

but brushed off Pharaoh and his army into the Red Sea—

To him who made his people travel through the wilderness—

To him who struck down great kings, For his mercy endures
forever.

18 and killed mighty kings,

Sihon king of the Amorites, For his mercy endures forever.

20 and Og king of Bashan, For his mercy endures forever.

and gave their land as a possession,

a possession to his servant Israel. For his mercy endures forever.

Who remembered us in our low condition,

and tore us out of the hands of our oppressors.

He gives food to all living creatures.[b]

Give thanks to the God of the heavens. For his mercy endures
forever.

Made in the USA
Monee, IL
05 July 2024

61242290R00184